Super Cheap Singapore Travel Guide 2021

Our Mission

Like Simon Sinek said, "People don't buy what you do; they buy why you do it". We believe strongly that travel can and is best enjoyed on a budget.

Taking a trip to Singapore is not just an outer journey, it's an inner one. Budget travel brings us closer to locals, culture and authenticity; which in turn makes our inner journeys more peaceful.

Travelling is painted as an expensive hobby; Travel guides, Travel bloggers and influencers often show you overpriced accommodation, restaurants and big-ticket attractions because they make money from our 'we're on vacation' mentality which leads to reckless spending. Our mission is to teach you how to enjoy more for less and get the best value from every dollar you spend in Singapore.

This guide focuses on the cheap or free in Singapore, but there is little value in travelling to Singapore and not experiencing all it has to offer. Where possible we've included cheap workarounds or listed the experience in the loved but costly section - if it is worth your time and money.

We work to dispel myths, save you tons of money, teach you the local tips and tricks and help you find experiences in Singapore that will flash before your eyes when you come to take your last breath on this beautiful earth.

Who this book is for and why anyone can enjoy budget travel

I've been travelling full-time for 20 years. I don't have a job and I'm not in any debt, which prompts friends and family to ask 'How can you afford to travel?'. My response? 'My passion is finding travel bargains'. This doesn't mean I do any less or sleep in dirty hostels. Someone who spends A LOT on travel hasn't planned or wants to spend their money. I believe you can live the bougie life on a budget; that's what I've been doing for the past 20 years.

Together with thrifty locals I met along the way I have funnelled my passion for travel bargains into 300 travel guides. In this guide, we have formulated a system to pass on to you, so you too can juice everything from visiting Singapore while spending the least possible money.

There is a big difference between being cheap and frugal. I like to spend money on beautiful experiences, but 20 years of travel has taught me I could have a 20 cent experience that will stir my soul more than a $100 one. Of course, there are times when the reverse is true, my point is, spending money on travel is the best investment you can make but it doesn't have to be at levels set by hotels and attractions with massive ad spends and influencers who are paid small fortunes to get you to buy into something that you could have for a fraction of the cost.

I love travelling because it forces me to be present-minded. I like to have the cold hard budget busting facts to hand (which is why we've included so many one page charts, which you can use as a quick reference), but otherwise, I want to shape my own experience - and I'm sure you do too.

We have designed these travel guides to give you a unique planning tool to experience an unforgettable trip without spending the ascribed tourist budget.

When it comes to FUN budget travel, it's all about what you know. You can have all the feels without most of the bills. A few days spent planning can save you thousands. Luckily, Super Cheap Insider Guides have done the planning for you, so you can distill the information in minutes not days, leaving you to focus on what matters: immersing yourself in the sights, sounds and smells of Singapore, meeting awesome new people and most importantly, feeling relaxed and happy. My sincere hope is that our tips will bring you great joy at a fraction of the price you expected.

So, grab a cup of tea, put your feet up and relax; you're about to enter the world of enjoying Singapore on the cheap. Oh and don't forget a biscuit. You need energy to plan a trip of a lifetime on a budget.

Super Cheap Singapore is <u>not</u> for travellers with the following needs:

1. You require a book with detailed offline travel maps. Super Cheap Insider Guides are best used with Google Maps - download and star our recommendations before you travel to make the most of your time and money.
2. You would like thousands of accommodation, food and attraction recommendations; by definition, cheapest is most often singular. We only include maximum value recommendations. We purposively leave out over-priced attractions when there is no workaround.
3. You would like detailed write-ups about hotels/Airbnbs/Restaurants. We are bargain hunters first and foremost. We dedicate our time to finding the best deals, not writing flowery language about their interiors. Plus things change. If I had a pound for every time I'd read a Lonely Planet description only to find the place completely different, I would be a rich man. Always look at online reviews for the latest up to date information.

If you want to save A LOT of money while comfortably enjoying an unforgettable trip to Singapore, minus the marketing, hype, scams and tourist traps read on.

Redefining Super Cheap

The value you get out of Super Cheap Singapore is not based on what you paid for it; its based on what you do with it. You can only do great things with it, if you believe saving money is worth your time. Charging things to your credit card and thinking 'oh I'll pay it off when I get back' is something you won't be tempted to do if you change your beliefs now. Think about what you associate with the word cheap, because you make your beliefs and your beliefs make you.

I grew up thinking you had to spend more than you could afford to have a good time travelling. Now I've visited 190 countries I know nothing is further from the truth. Before you embark upon reading our specific tips for Singapore think about your associations with the word cheap.

Here are the dictionary definitions of cheap:

1.   costing very little; relatively low in price; inexpensive:
a cheap dress.
2.   costing little labor or trouble:
Words are cheap.
3.   charging low prices:
a very cheap store.
4.   **of little account; of small value; mean; shoddy:**
cheap conduct; cheap workmanship.
5.   **embarrassed; sheepish:**
He felt cheap about his mistake.
6.   **stingy; miserly:**
He's too cheap to buy his own brother a cup of coffee.

Three out of six definitions have extremely negative connotations. The 'super cheap' we're talking about in this book is not shoddy, embarrassed or stingy. We donate 10% of our book profits to charity (details of the charities we support are at the end of the book) so you've already donated to charity just by buying this book - how is that stingy?

We added the super to reinforce our message. Super's dictionary definition stands for 'a super quality'. Super Cheap stands for enjoying the best on the lowest budget. Question other peoples definitions of cheap so you're not blinded to possibilities, potential, and prosperity. Here are some new associations to consider forging:

Shoddy

Cheap stuff doesn't last is an adage marketing companies have drilled into consumers. However by asking vendors the right questions cheap doesn't mean something won't last, I had a $10 backpack last for 8 years and a $100 suitcase bust on the first journey. A study out of San Francisco University found that people who spent money on experiences rather than things were happier. Memories last forever, not things, even expensive things. And as we will show you during this guide you don't need to pay to create great memories.

Embarrassed

I have friends who routinely pay more to vendors because they think their money is putting food on this person's table. Paradoxically, Cuban doctors are driving taxi's because they earn more money; it's not always a good thing for the place you're visiting to pay more and can cause unwanted distortion in their culture - Airbnb pushing out renters is an obvious example. Think carefully about whether the extra money is helping people or incentivising greed.

Stingy

Cheap can be eco-friendly. Buying thrift clothes is cheap but you also help the Earth. Many travellers are often disillusioned by the reality of traveling experience since the places on our bucketlists are overcrowded. Cheap can take you away from the crowds. You can find balance and harmony being cheap. Remember,"A journey is best measured in friends, rather than miles." – Tim Cahill. And making friends is free!

A recent survey by Credit Karma found 50% of Millennials and Gen Z get into debt travelling. **Please don't allow credit card debt to be an unwanted souvenir you take home.** As you will see from this book, there's so much you can enjoy in Singapore for free and so many ways to save money! You just need to want to!

Discover Singapore

Singapore attract 18 million visitors annually. Many of them come to try the Incredible local food that has emerged from the eclectic mix of cultures. Among the best are chilli crab and laksa.

Modern Singapore was founded in 1819 by Sir Stamford Raffles (1781-1826) but evidence suggests Singapore was settled as early as the third century. A significant trading settlement was established in the 14 century. It's clear Singapore has long been a melting pot of Asian and Western cultures. In Singapore values merge, you'll see Chinese, Malay, Indian, Eurasian and Caucasian faces harmoniously living side by side. This meshing of cultures has given rise to eclectic lifestyles; Singapore is Asia with all its colour and flavour, the only difference being here you'll find more comfort and increasingly exciting street food combinations.

144 years' of British rule over Singapore ended on 16 September 1963 when Singapore became part of Malaysia. Due to political and economical disputes two years later on 9 August 1965, Singapore left Malaysia and became an independent Republic.

Today Singapore is a city-state, famous for its draconian rules, chewing gum ban, Confucius inspired fines for littering, spitting and other social faux-pars. It's South-East Asia's most important financial centre. But don't be fooled by its sterile image Singapore offers a beach, skyline and a patchwork of endlessly engrossing neighbourhoods to lose yourself in.

A trip to Singapore will clean the cobwebs from your soul, but it doesn't have to empty the cash from your wallet. Due to the sheer number of big ticket attractions Singapore has the reputation of being among the most luxurious and expensive destinations in the world. Fortunately, some of the best things in life are free (or almost free). The trick to keeping your trip affordable is to get off the tourist track and find the local deals and thats exactly what this guide will show you!

INSIDER HISTORICAL INSIGHT

Singapore's name is part legend part fairytale. It comes from the Sanskrit 'Singa Pura' which means Lion City. In the 17th century a Sumatran prince landed on Temasek (the old name of Singapore). He saw a Lion, called 'Singa' in Malay. And thus Singapore was renamed. Many people believe The Lion City was actually inspired by a tiger because there were no records of lions. While tigers were found in Singapore up until the 1930s.

Some of Singapore's Best Bargains

Skip the Singapore Flyer

Skip the Singapore Flyer which costs S$33. Instead, for amazing views over the city, head to the 50th-floor rooftop of Pinnacle@Duxton - the worlds largest public housing complex. You can go to the top for bargain S$6.

If you don't want to splurge the S$6, behind the National Gallery Singapore is the glass fronted New Supreme Court 5. It has a FREE observation deck on the 8th floor with stunning views.

Visit Jurong Lake

The gardens incorporate the existing Chinese Garden and Japanese Garden and they are totally free to enjoy!

Do a Singapore River Cruise on the cheap

Take a commuter boat on weekdays; see www.rivercruise.com.sg for stops and times. Tickets are 90% cheaper than traditional river cruises.

Get a 20min foot reflexology for S$10

Mr Lim Foot Reflexology in People's Park Complex offers an incomparably good foot massage for S$10.

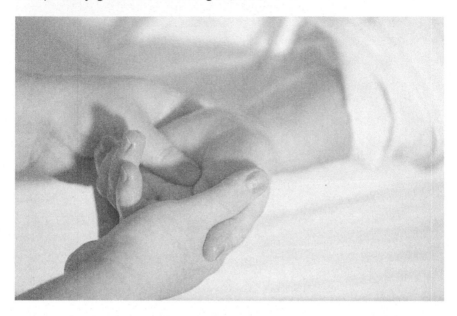

Enjoy upscale food on the cheap

The Halia at Singapore Botanic Gardens offers a cheap weekday set lunch for S$28, just $18. Make sure you're seated on the outside to have the best experience.

Visit the world's highest alfresco bar

Altitude Rooftop Gallery & Bar is 282m above street level, with stunning 360-degree panoramic views. Women can get a particularly good deal, with free entry and S$10 martinis on Wednesdays. Which is cheap by Singapore drinking standards. Dress fancy if you plan to go.

If you're looking for good deals on drinks make the most of happy hours, usually between 5pm and 9pm. Cook & Brew is one of Singapore's best happy hour joints with half-price drinks.

Planning your trip

When to visit?

The first step in saving money on your Singapore trip is timing. Singapore is hot and humid year round with average temperatures of 28°C. Rain is very common, the wettest months are during the monsoon season: November to January. July to August are the best months to visit as they're the country's tourist low-season. The humidity makes everything sticky so pack linen and lighter loose clothes.

Mid-September is when the Singapore Grand Prix takes place. Book your accommodation at least three months ahead if you plan to visit during this time.

Where to stay?

This is a personal preference and should be based on your interests and what attractions you plan to visit. If you're travelling solo, Singapore hostels are your best option, both for meeting people and saving pennies. Tree In Lodge is in the heart of Singapore and provides a solid base with free breakfast. Dorms come in at $12 a night.

Airbnbs are cheapest if you're more than one person, you don't need to pay for dorm beds. Plus you can cook some of your meals and enjoy more privacy. If you're travelling as part of a group you can score a private room in an Airbnb in the heart of downtown Singapore for $30 - https://www.airbnb.com/rooms/10598600?s=67&shared_item_-type=1&virality_entry_point=1&sharer_id=4035262

If using Airbnb in Singapore, be sure to check for three things:
- a track record of good reviews,
- a good location relative to the MRT.
- read the complete description. There's nothing more annoying than buying food to cook and finding there's no stove or oven.

The best price performance location in Singapore

A room putting Singapore's attractions, restaurants, and nightlife within walking distance will save you time and money on transport. However restaurants and bars get much cheaper the further you go from famous tourist attractions. You will also get a better idea of the day to day life of a local if you stay on a road like Selegie Road in Little India either in a last-minute hotel, Airbnb or hostel.

If you want a private room check out budget hotels in Geylang, they're usually much cheaper than anywhere else. Geylang gets a bad rep as it's the 'red light district' but it's safe. Singapore is one of the safest places on the planet. The advantage of Geylang is that there is lots of great cheap food nearby, its close to MRT and direct buses into town (about 20 mins to orchard road). My visitors always stay at the Fragrance Emerald, some of the other Fragrance branches are a bit run down but Emerald is newly refurbished and very clean. You can always get rooms for around sgd$70/ for a night, $50 USD.

Q Loft Hotels@Mackenzie is a luxurious 3-star hotel a bit further out with consistent last-minute rooms from $30 a night. Hotel 1887 is another 3-star hotel in Chinatown with consistent last-minute rooms from $60.

How to ensure your travel insurance covers you for COVID-19

Many insurers stopped selling travel insurance after the start of the pandemic, some have returned with some form of 'COVID-19 cover'. MoneySupermarket.com is updating a list of insurers who cover you for varying degrees of pandemic-related travel disruption. Check on their website before buying a policy to avoid having to wade through the fine print - much of which is not written in plain English and may contain degrees of pandemic coverage such as they will pay your medical expenses but not your flight home. Book hotels and flights with a credit card that cover pandemic-related travel expenses for an added level of security.

REMEMBER if you travel to a country your government is currently advising against travel to for your planned dates, then it's likely that you won't be covered at all.

Singapore's Neighbourhoods

Arab Street, Kampong

Kampong Glam
Kampong Glam is Singapore's Muslim Quarter. Here you will find 19th-century shophouses centred around busy Arab Street that have been turned into stores selling textiles and casual eateries. It's home to the Sultan Mosque and the Malay Heritage Centre and some of the best street art in the city.

Geylang
Originally home to the 'Orange Laut' (seapeople and Malays) Geylang is among Singapore's biggest Malay districts - 150,000 Singaporeans call it home. Here you'll find the 'Malay Village' - where you can see how the Malays lived in the 50s and 60s. Unfortunately as stated above, its is also home to Singapore's red light district and most tourists avoid it, but its safe, cheap and offers great food.

Little India

Fancy an electric shock to your senses? Walk down the main road - Dunlop Street, you will discover a hypnotic dose of colours, sounds and scents. f you like a bustling vibe, go on Sunday evening when thousands of local men enjoy their days off in the parks, streets and lanes.

Changi
Changi is where you go to escape the metropolis. It's on the east coast and the closest thing you'll get to old Singapore. There's lots of lovely nature trails to explore.

Chinatown
Despite the constant invitation to buy something, Chinatown is a hub of activity and home to the mesmerising Sri Mariamman Temple.

Raffles Place
Skyscrapers and shopping merge at the most visited place in Singapore: Raffles Place. It was planned and developed in the 1820s as a commercial centre and is still thriving as one today.

Hack your Singapore Accommodation

Your two biggest expenses when travelling to Singapore are accommodation and food. This section is intended to help you cut these costs dramatically before and while you are in Singapore.

Hostels are the cheapest accommodation in Singapore but there are some creative workarounds to upgrade your stay on the cheap.

Use Time

There are two ways to use time. One is to book in advance. Three months will net you the best deal, especially if your visit coincides with an event. The other is to book on the day of your stay. This is a risky move, but if executed well, you can lay your head in a five-star hotel for a 2-star fee.

Before you travel to Singapore, check for big events using a simple google search 'What's on in Singapore', if you find no big events drawing travellers, risk showing up with no accommodation booked (If there are big events on, demand exceeds supply and you should avoid using this strategy). Start checking for discount rooms at 11 am using a private browser on booking.com.

Before I go into demand-based pricing, take a moment to think about your risk tolerance. By risk, I am not talking about personal safety. No amount of financial savings is worth risking that. What I am talking about is being inconvenienced. Do you deal well with last-minute changes? Can you roll with the punches or do you freak out if something changes? Everyone is different and knowing yourself is the best way to plan a great trip. If you are someone that likes to have everything pre-planned using demand-based pricing to get cheap accommodation will not work for you. Skip this section and go to blind-booking.

Demand-based pricing

Be they an Airbnb host or hotel manager; no one wants empty rooms. Most will do anything to make some revenue because they still have the same costs to cover whether the room is occupied or not. That's why you will find many hotels drastically slashing room rates for same-day bookings.

How to book five-star hotels for a two-star price

You will not be able to find these discounts when the demand exceeds the supply. So if you're visiting during the peak season, or during an event which has drawn many travellers again don't try this.

On the day of your stay, visit booking.com (which offers better discounts than Kayak and agoda.com). Hotel Tonight individually checks for any last-minute bookings, but they take a big chunk of the action, so the better deals come from booking.com. The best results come from booking between 2 pm and 4 pm when the risk of losing any revenue with no occupancy is most pronounced, so algorithms supporting hotels slash prices. This is when you can find rates that are not within the "lowest publicly visible" rate. To avoid losing customers to other websites, or cheapening the image of their hotel most will only offer the super cheap rates during a two hour window from 2 pm to 4 pm. Two guests will pay 10x difference in price but it's absolutely vital to the hotel that neither knows it.

Takeaway: To get the lowest price book on the day of stay between 2 pm and 4 pm and extend your search radius to include further afield hotels with good transport connections.

How to trick travel Algorithms to get the lowest hotel price

Do not believe anyone who says changing your IP address to get cheaper hotels or flights does NOT work. If you don't believe us, download a Tor Network and search for flights and hotels to one destination using your current IP and then the tor network (a tor browser hides your IP address from algorithms. It is commonly used by hackers because websites can't track or predict behaviours). You will receive different prices.

The price you see is a decision made by an algorithm that adjusts prices using data points such as past bookings, remaining capacity, average demand and the probability of selling the room or flight later at a higher price. If booking.com knows you've searched for the area before it will keep the prices high. To circumvent this, you can either use a different IP address from a cafe or airport or data from an international sim. I use a sim from Three, which provides free data in many countries around the world. When you search from a new IP address, most of the time, and particularly near booking you will get a lower price. Sometimes if your sim comes from a 'rich' country, say the UK or USA, you will see higher rates as the algorithm has learnt people from these countries pay more. The solution is to book from a local wifi connection - but a different one from the one you originally searched from.

How to get last-minute discounts on owner rented properties

In addition to Airbnb, you can also find owner rented rooms and apartments on www.vrbo.com or HomeAway or a host of others. Nearly all owners renting accommodation will happily give renters a "last-minute" discount to avoid the space sitting empty, not earning a dime.

Go to Airbnb or another platform and put in today's date. Once you've found something you like start the negotiating by asking for a 25% reduction. A sample message to an Airbnb host might read:

Dear HOST NAME,

I love your apartment. It looks perfect for me. Unfortunately, I'm on a very tight budget. I hope you won't be offended, but I wanted to ask if you would be amenable to offering me a 25% discount for tonight, tomorrow and the following day? I see that you aren't booked. I can assure you, I will leave your place exactly the way I found it. I will put bed linen in the washer and ensure everything is clean for the next guest. I would be delighted to bring you a bottle of wine to thank you for any discount that you could offer.

If this sounds okay, please send me a custom offer, and I will book immediately.

YOUR NAME.

A polite, genuine message like this, that proposes reciprocity will be successful 80% of the time. Don't ask for more than 25% off, this person still has to pay the bills and will probably say no as your stay will cost them more in bills than they make. Plus starting higher, can offend the owner. Do you want to stay somewhere, where you have offended the host?

In Practice

To use either of these methods, you must travel light. Less stuff means greater mobility, everything is faster and you don't have to check-in or store luggage. If you have a lot of luggage, you're going to have fewer opportunities to save on accommodation. Plus travelling light benefits the planet - you're buying, consuming, and transporting less.

Blind-booking

If your risk tolerance does not allow for last-minute booking, you can use blind-booking. Many hotels in Singapore not wanting to cheapen their brand with known low-prices, choose to operate a blind booking policy. This is where you book without knowing the name of the hotel you're going to stay in until you've made the payment. This is also sometimes used as a marketing strategy where the hotel is seeking to recover from past issues (commonly bad reviews from poor service). As long as you choose 4 or 5 star hotels, you will find them to be clean, comfortable and safe. priceline.com, Hot Rate® Hotels and Top Secret Hotels (operated by lastminute.com) offer the best deals in Singapore.

Hotels.com Loyalty Program

This is currently the best hotel loyalty program with hotels in Singapore. The basic premise is you collect 10 nights and get 1 free. hotels.com price match, so if booking.com has a cheaper price you can get hotel.com, to match. If you intend to travel more than ten nights in a year, its a great choice to get the 11th free.

Don't let time use you.

Rigidity will cost you money. You pay the price you're willing to pay, not the amount it requires a hotel to deliver. Therefore if you're in town for a big event, saving money on accommodation is nearly impossible so in such cases book three months ahead.

Use our FREE accommodation find-er service

Feeling overwhelmed by all the accommodation options in Singapore? Save yourself the stress, hassle and time by using our FREE accommodation finder service.

We pride ourselves on actively helping our readers find the best price-performance accommodation. We normally charge $50 for this service, but for our paid readers it is FREE when you leave an honest review of this book. (Just a few short words like 'Good budget tips and insider insights' is all it takes).

So, how do you use the service?

Simply send our Services Manager, Amy Abraham the following information:

1. A screenshot proof of purchase. (Go to your Amazon account, and click orders and make a screenshot of your purchase.)
2. Send a screenshot of your review of the guide on Amazon.
3. Send answers to the following questions:

* What's your Budget? (e.g. lowest possible)
* How many are travelling and what are their ages? (e.g. do you need a baby bed?)
* What Approximate location do you desire? (e.g. as close to the centre as possible/ near public transport)
* Do you have a strong dislike of either hostels or Airbnbs?

- If anyone in your group has mobility restrictions/ requires a lift/ no stairs etc?
- Add any details you think are pertinent to your needs.

About Amy and her team

Amy has travelled to over 170 countries personally and has recruited a team of bargain hunters to provide our accommodation finder service.

Send your details via E-mail to Amy Abraham at Amy@supercheapinsiderguides.com

Make a request via Facebook

We also accept accommodation search requests via Facebook messenger, just make sure you send the necessary information listed above. You can find us here: https://www.facebook.com/SuperCheapInsiderGuides/

What you'll receive

Amy and her team will work their magic. Within 24 hours you will be sent a list of the top three accommodations for your specific needs prioritised by which one we recommend.

(Please note: If you received this book for free as part of a promotion, we cannot extend this service to you.)

We offer the same service for finding you the cheapest most direct flight. See our cheapest route to Singapore for details.

How to be a green tourist in Singapore

Singapore like other major cities struggles with high levels of air pollution, so it's important as responsible tourists that we help not hinder Singapore. There is a bizarre misconception that you have to spend money to travel in an eco-friendly way. This like, all marketing myths was concocted and hyped by companies seeking to make money. Anything with eco in front of their names e.g Eco-tours will be triple the cost of the regular tour. Don't get me wrong, sometimes its best to take these tours if you're visiting endangered areas. However, in most instances such places have extensive legislation that everyone, including the eco and non-eco tour companies must comply with. The vast majority of ways you can travel eco-friendly are free and even save you money:

- Avoid Bottled Water - get a good water bottle and refill. Unlike other Asian cities, the water in Singapore is safe to drink.
- Thrift shop but check the labels and don't buy polyester clothes. Overtime plastic is released into the ocean when we wash polyester.
- Don't put it in a plastic bag, bring a cotton tote with you when you venture out.
- Pack Light - this is one of the best ways to save money. If you find a 5-star hotel for tonight for $10, and you're at an Airbnb or hostel, you can easily pack and upgrade hassle-free. A light pack equals freedom and it means less to wash.
- Travel around Singapore on Bikes or e-Scooters or use Public Transportation.
- Car Pool with services like bla bla car or Uber/Lyft share.

- Walk, this is the best way to get to know Singapore. You never know what's around the corner!
- Travel Overland - this isn't always viable especially if you only have limited time off work, but where possible avoid flying and if you have to compensate by off-setting or keeping the rest of your trip carbon-neutral by doing all of the above.

Saving money on Singapore Food

Eat at Hawker Centres

Hawker centres are open-air complexes selling cheap food. Often found in air-conditioned shopping malls. Maxwell hawker centre and Chinatown Complex Food Centre

Breakfast

If you stay somewhere with a free breakfast, eat smart. Don't eat sugary cereals or white flour rich pastries if you don't want to be hungry an hour later. Before leaving your hotel or checking out, find some fresh fruit, water, and granola in the fitness centre or coffee in the lobby or business centre. If your hotel doesn't have free breakfast, never take it. You can always eat cheaper outside. The Hangar has the best cheap breakfast we found. Here you can pick up a tasty breakfast for less than $3.

Visit supermarkets at discount times.

You can get a 50 per cent discount around 5 pm at the Fair Price supermarkets on fresh produce. The cheaper the supermarket, the less discounts you will find. The biggest discount in Fair Price are found at 5 pm. Some items are also marked down due to sell-by date after the lunchtime rush so if you happen to pass a Fair Price check inside for lunchtime discounts.

Use delivery services on the cheap.

Take advantage of local offers on food delivery services. Most platforms including Food Panda offer $10 off the first order in Singapore.

Before we begin here is a snapshot of how you can enjoy a $1,000 trip to Singapore for $150

A fully costed breakdown will be explained at the end of this guide.

Stay	You can find Private room on airbnb for $14 in the city. Here is the link to a perfect Airbnb: https://www.airbnb.com/rooms/6813505?s=51,
	Stay in hostels if you want to meet over travellers. The best price performance hostel is Tree In Lodge hostel.
	Or there's the option to use our free accommodation finder service.
Eat	You don't need to spend a fortune in Singapore to eat memorable food. Average meal cost: $5 – $15
Move	Cycle $3 a day
See	Free museums, galleries,, markets, beaches,
Total	US$150

Unique Bargains I love in Singapore

Buddha Tooth Relic Temple And Museum In Singapore.

Just walking through Chinatown (great cheap food on smith street), get lost around Little India, wander around Arab Street, check out the Colonial district and the Marina bay, Fireworks At The Crane Dance (Sentosa), Siloso beach / Palawan beach (Sentosa) and Walk from Vivo city to Sentosa via the Sentosa boardwalk (it's free), Orchard road, and make sure you take a stroll through boat quay and Clarke quay, especially at night. Plus exploring The gardens by the bay, the botanical gardens, Sentosa + beaches, MacRitchie park and treetop walk, and Palau Ubin is all free! With all these fabulous free ways to entertain yourself even the most reluctant bargain hunter can be successful in Singapore.

The first thing you should do when you arrive is check https://www.eventbrite.com/d/singapore--singapore/free--events/ to see what free events are on. Plus if you're in need of anything (clothes, bag, pens) events give out amazing free stuff every day.

Singapore is expensive, but the hawker centres have some of the best food in the world for very very low prices. Some of the best hawker centres are in the DBS area. It's 15 minutes walk from MBS, near China Town and Clarke Quay. Lau Pa Sat is also a great place to grab a cheap lunch and has amazing food all-day long and relatively cheap beer. There's so much to experience cheaply you'll be planning your next trip to Singapore!

If you have one, Take your student card
Singapore offers hundreds of student discounts. If you're studying buy an ISIC card - International Student Identity Card. It's a great investment because its valid in 133 countries and covers 150,000 discounts including many hundreds in Singapore.

How to use this book

Google and TripAdvisor are your on-the-go guides while travelling, a travel guide adds the most value during the planning phase, and if you're without wifi. Always download the google map for your destination - having an offline map will make using Super Cheap Singapore much more comfortable. For ease of use, we've set the book out the way you travel starting with arriving, how to get around, then on to the money-saving tips. The tips we ordered according to when you need to know the tip to save money, so free tours and combination tickets feature first. We prioritised the rest of the tips by how much money you can save and by how likely it was that you would be able to find the tip with a google search. Meaning those we think you could find alone are nearer the bottom. I hope you find this layout useful. If you have any ideas about making Super Cheap Insider Guides easy to use, please email me philgtang@gmail.com

A quick note on how we Source Super Cheap Tips

We focus entirely on finding the best bargains. We give each of our collaborators $2,000 to hunt down never-before-seen deals. The type you either only know if you're local or by on the ground research. The actual writing and editing are done for free by four people (see who are writers are at the end of the book). As we grow, we will hire more writers to pen fabulous prose, but for now, we are in the nuts and bolts of hunting down unbelievable deals. We do this yearly, which means we just keep finding more amazing ways for you to have the same experience for less, but that's also why if you read or listen more of our guides, you may find the sentence structure familiar. Like many other guide book companies (Lonely Planet, Rough Guides etc) we use a content management system (ie, we repurpose some text). We'd like to be upfront about this so if you read or listen to another of our guides you aren't annoyed. Its worth mentioning that we pride ourselves on being a hands-on travel guide, and we put substantial resource behind helping you find the cheapest flight (explained in a moment) and the best value accommodation.

Another way you can save and make money is to apply to become one of our local collaborators at supercheapinsiderguides.com. We require you to identify a minimum of 250 super cheap tips and you need to live in the area you research. When you hear INSIDER HISTORICAL INSIGHT or INSIDER CULTURAL INSIGHT or INSIDER MONEY SAVING TIP this is a specific tip our insider contributed. Now let's get started with juicing the most pleasure from your trip to Singapore with the least possible money.

Our super cheap tips

Here are our specific super cheap tips for enjoying a $1,000 trip to Singapore for just $150.

Cheapest route to Singapore from America

At the time of writing Xiamen Air are flying for around $460 return out of LA. Phil's day job for the past 15 years has

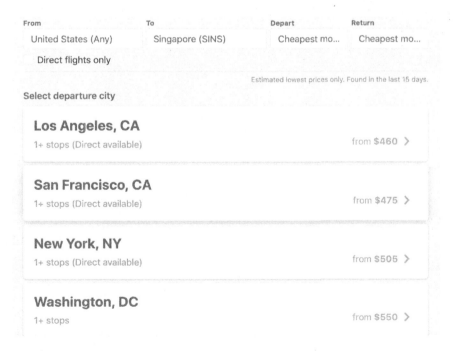

From	To	Depart	Return
United States (Any)	Singapore (SINS)	Cheapest mo...	Cheapest mo...
Direct flights only			

Estimated lowest prices only. Found in the last 15 days.

Select departure city

Los Angeles, CA
1+ stops (Direct available) — from $460 >

San Francisco, CA
1+ stops (Direct available) — from $475 >

New York, NY
1+ stops (Direct available) — from $505 >

Washington, DC
1+ stops — from $550 >

been finding cheap flights for blue chip companies, so if

you need help finding a cheap flight Phil can help you for free. Simply review this book and send him an email. philgtang@gmail.com (Please send a screenshot of your review - with your flight hacking request). Phil aims to reply to you within 12 hours. If it's an urgent request mark the email URGENT in the subject line and he will endeavour to reply ASAP.

Cheapest route to Singapore from Europe

At the time of writing the cheapest route is from Berlin with . KLM for around $336 return. Always buy a return for long distances as it works out cheaper.

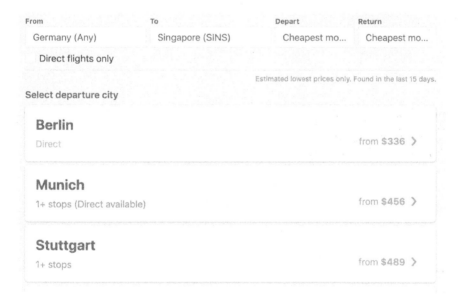

From	To	Depart	Return
Germany (Any)	Singapore (SINS)	Cheapest mo...	Cheapest mo...
Direct flights only			

Estimated lowest prices only. Found in the last 15 days.

Select departure city

Berlin
Direct   from $336 >

Munich
1+ stops (Direct available)   from $456 >

Stuttgart
1+ stops   from $489 >

If you are flying to Singapore from anywhere else, Phil can also help you find the cheapest, most direct flight for free.

Arriving

The Cheapest way from the airport to the city is to take the MRT to the city centre. Transfer to the westbound train at Tanah Merah Station (3rd station from Changi Airport on the Green line). The Last train leaves from Changi Airport at 11:18 pm and the first trains depart at 5:30 or 6:30am on Sundays.

If your accommodation is in Chinatown, Little India, Clarke Quay, and Farrer Park travel to Outram Park (Green Line), then transfer to the North East bound train (Violet line).

Otherwise find the nearest MRT station to your hotel.

INSIDER MONEY SAVING TIP

To use the MRT buy an ez-link card either at the MRT stations or 7-Eleven stores. Cards sold at the stations costs $12, out of which $7 is valid for use. Cards sold at 7-Eleven cost $10, out of which $5 is valid for use.

INSIDER CULTURAL INSIGHT

The Singapore chewing gum ban has been in place since 1992. Since 2004, an exception has been made for medical gum. Tourists are allowed to bring in up to two packs of chewing gum per person but heavy fines apply if you drop gum on the streets.

Getting around

Transport is a cost that can quickly add up but there are ways to save while exploring Singapore:

Cycle
Like a growing number of cities around the world, Singapore has a bike-sharing program. Theres no deposit and you can unlock with EZ-Link card: https://www.sgbike.com.sg/. The first 30 minutes are free. It's $0.03 per minute after the first 30 minutes. Just beware there are no cycle lanes in Singapore, as long as you're vigilant and or stick to the more scenic routes like East Coast Park, it will be an enjoyable experience. A ride to Marina Barrage will bring you amazing views of the Singapore skyline and Marina area. oBike is another provider but they charge you $1.99 for 30 minutes.

E-scooters - Bird are the biggest providers, but prices are high. It works out much cheaper to bike.

Walk – it's the best way to discover. Some parts of Singapore are within walking distance of each other, such as Boat Quayand Chinatown. The best places to explore on foot are around Clarke quay, little India, China town, Arab Town. Head down to Haji Lane. Go café-hopping at Tiong Bahru to find the best coffee and pastries. Just take a walk around Yong Siak Street or Eng Hoon Street, and you'll be able to find a cute café on every corner. It's a very walkable country with great architecture. Unfortunately, for the main tourist sights you'll have to use public transport more than once to see them all.

By MRT (Mass Rapid Transit): Singapore's rail system, operates both over and underground. Its fast, safe and easy. There are three lines in operation. The best time to use public transport is during the middle of the day when the sun it's at its strongest. The best bang for your buck is to

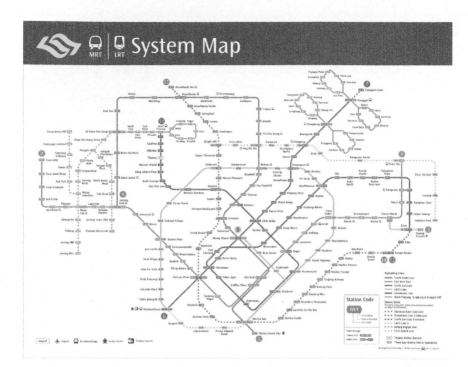

buy a 2 day unlimited tourist pass for S$16 ($11 USD). Avoid traveling on MRT around peak hour period- 7-9am & 5-7pm.

Kids under 0.9m tall can also ride the MRT for free.

Grab will stop you being conned

Grab is mostly 3 times cheaper than a local taxi. The price is set and you can't be ripped off by an opportunistic driver because you don't know the regular fare. Download grab and follow sg-code on Instagram for promo code discounts.

💡 INSIDER MONEY SAVING TIP

- -

Driving is extremely expensive in Singapore and not rec-ommended. If you're planning on renting a car always re-serve the cheapest car and rent at the Singapore airport.

They usually run out of them first. And if they do, you'll be upgraded to a bigger and better vehicle at no additional cost.

SAVE $$$ ON GAS!
Visit www.gasbuddy.com, www.gaspricewatch.com, and www.fuelmeup.com to find the cheapest
gas prices in Singapore.

You can park at the Mustafa Centre for free for the first hour. $2 thereafter. This is the cheapest parking in central Singapore... we warned you its expensive.

Orientate yourself with this free tour

Forget exploring Singapore by wandering around aimlessly. Start with a free organised tour. Nothing compares to local advice, especially when travelling on a budget. Ask for their recommendations for the best cheap eats, the best bargains, the best markets, the best place for a particular street eat. Perhaps some of it will be repeated from this guide, but it can't hurt to ask, especially if you have specific needs or questions. At the end you should leave an appropriate tip (usually around $5), but nobody bats an eye lid if you are unable or unwilling to do so, tell them you will leave a good review and always give them a little gift from home - I always carry small Vienna fridge magnets and I always tip the $5, but it is totally up to you.

This is the free tour we recommend. It's a great introduction to the city and covers all the main attractions. You can book here: http://www.copenhagenfreewalkingtours.dk/in-dex.html

A note on paying for tours

The only time paying for a tour is worth it, is when you couldn't reach the place without the tour (e.g you need a boat), or when the tour is about the same price as the attraction entry. Otherwise you can do a range of self-guided tours using gpsmycity.com for FREE.

 INSIDER MONEY SAVING TIP

----

if you have more time Try Geocaching. This is where you hunt for hide-and-seek containers. You need a mobile device to follow the GPS clues in Singapore. A typical cache is a small, waterproof container with a logbook where you can leave a message or see various trinkets left by other cache hunters. Build your own treasure hunt by discovering geocaches in Singapore. www.geocaching.com

Visit Singapore's Museums for Free

Many of Singapore's top museums are free and others have free entry times to ensure that culture can be accessed by everyone. Here are the best of the free crop you can visit:

Remember to go early on the free days to avoid the crowds, and pack snacks to avoid paying the inflated food prices at museum cafes.

Singapore Art Museum - the world's largest public collection of modern and contemporary Southeast Asian art. Save $10 on the entry fee and go for free on Friday evenings between 6pm and 9pm.

Museums & Galleries Baba House

You have to book ahead (https://babahouse.nus.edu.sg/) but its worth it for a free, guided tour of one of Singapore's most elegantly restored Peranakan homes. The 100 year old house is culturally and historically rich, full of colour, symbol and meaning, A wonderful glimpse into the past made even more interesting by the wonderful and informative Baba House guides. No photos allowed inside.

Old Hill Street Police Station

The multicoloured building on the corner of Hill St is the Old Hill Street Police Station, it opened in 1934 and was home to the police and many of their family members. It's beautifully designed and free to go inside to explore the stories. The building is close to Fort Canning Park and The Clarke Quay.

Parkview Museum

Huge contemporary art museum opened in 2017. It's free, open daily even on weekends. No queue and usually only 2 or 3 people inside. The pieces are arresting and you could easily lose a blissful afternoon here.

Red Dot Design Museum Singapore

Design and communication design museum named after the major prize, covering AI to clothing, data representation to robotics. Its a nice way to spend an hour or two, especially if you've an interest in design and/or tech Pay as you wish. Free admission for children six years and under.

Buddha Tooth Relic Temple & Museum in Chinatown

This Tang dynasty–style temple houses religious relics, with ornate rooms and a tranquil rooftop garden. Founded in 2002 by the venerable Shi Fazhao, this five-storey serene place of worship is dedicated to the Maitreya Buddha and rests one of Buddha's sacred body parts. Admission is free.

Important tip: Find the side door that leads to the upper levels of the temple and explore all the floors. The topmost floor is the one that contains the Buddha tooth relic in front of which is a space for meditation.

Republic of Singapore Air Force Museum
Experience what it's like to be a pilot. It is something for the family to do and explore for free.

The Gem Museum
Home to gems and minerals sourced from around the world, this private museum aims to educate the public about gemmology – and save you the misery of being scammed by gem fraudsters and its Free.

NUS Museum is free from Mon to Sat.
The NUS Museum is the oldest university museum in Singapore. There's an array of Asian/contemporary art pieces on display.

City Hall - The museum runs free one-hour tours through the galleries and also of the building's highlights. 20 slots are available on a first-come, first-served basis. Registration opens 20 minutes before each tour at the Tour Desk, B1 Concourse. https://www.nationalgallery.sg/about/building/architecture

INSIDER MONEY SAVING TIP

Be careful when Googling for free museums to visit in Singapore. Many will say they are free, but are in fact free for residents only and you will be asked to show your resident card.

Kids receive up to 50% discount at most tourist venues. Those aged six years and under enjoy free entry to many of Singapore's top museums, including the National Gallery Singapore, National Museum of Singapore and the Asian Civilisations Museum.

Enjoy a beach day on the cheap

Siloso Beach

When you need an escape from the busy metropolis, head to Sentosa Island to relax on the beach.

There are 3 beaches to choose from:

- Siloso beach is where you'll want to go for water and sports activities.
- Tanjong beach is a great spot to chill and enjoy a drink, and
- Palawan beach is where you'll go if you're traveling with kids.

The cheapest way here is to walk from Vivo city,
via Sentosa Boardwalk that connects Vivocity to Sentosa. It's totally free.

Taking the Monorail is S$4 per entry at the Sentosa Express station.

The cable car to Sentosa is not very scenic, and rather short ride for S$29 ($21) per person. Its a very marketed tourist activity but you can get a better experience walking. There are many cargo ships in the water here so don't expect the Thailand beach experience. The best thing to do around the beaches is explore on foot. Don't miss 'Nature Walk and Dragon's Trail' walk'.

INSIDER MONEY SAVING TIP

Visit Fort Siloso on Sentosa

Here you can learn about the British Surrender in 1942 and the Japanese Surrender in 1945. You can explore coastal guns and the remains of military structures around the compound. You can also explore Singapore in the late 1800s through a recreation of the Victorian Barrack Room. Admission is totally free.

Cheap alternative to The Singapore Flyer

The Equinox is a cheap alternative to Singapore Flyer for views. The Singapore flyer(the 65m-tall public observation wheel opened in 2008) costs $33 per adult $21 per kid, it is costly. For $45.00 you can get a afternoon tea at the equinox with tea and scones for two people

If you are thinking of splurging Singapore-style, enjoy amazing afternoon teas in the 5 star hotels. You can try some great rooftop bars like Ce La Vie, The Lantern, or 1-Altitude, but dress to impress.

INSIDER CULTURAL INSIGHT

How did Singapore get so rich?

Singapore has positioned itself for economic prosperity. First it provided the only sea route to China. Secondly, they negotiated a good deal with the British and third their political neutrality has proved rewarding.

Do the TreeTop walk

Take the bus to the TreeTop Walk at The MacRitchie Reservoir, get off at ESSO station where you can then head to Venus Drive to begin the treetop walk. The walk is free but don't feed the monkeys. Also don't NOT carry plastic bags or food, the monkeys will try to grab them. Make sure you put on a good amount of insect repellent before the walk.

The MacRitchie Trails are where the locals head for a run or a hike. After the treetop walk you can rent kayaks and canoes. The park is also home to rare flying lemurs - keep a look out!

The Southern Ridges also has forest canopy for strolling and breathtaking views. The entire walk can take between 3 to 5 hours. It is extremely well marked out and well laid out in the form of footpaths and walkways. Take bus 197 from Clementi MRT to "Opp Jin Tai Primary School" bus stop to begin the walk.

Enjoy Nature reserves

Sungei buloh mangrove

There are more than 300 parks in Singapore, but only four nature reserves: the Sungei Buloh Wetland Reserve, Bukit Timah, The Central Catchment Nature Reserve, and Labrador Nature Reserves. Entry to all is free.

Bukit Timah
This nature reserve is often abbreviated as Bt Timah. Here you'll find more plant species than in the whole of North America. It's a leafy, tropical nature reserve surrounding a hilltop with great walking trails and a free visitor center.

Wetland Reserve.
Home to a wide diversity of bird life, the park has hides to allow you to birdwatch. If you visit, make sure you walk through the mangrove forest.

The Central Catchment Nature Reserve
2880 hectares form a large green lung in the centre of the Singapore. Its a relaxing nature experience. There are a network of jungle trails where you can trek and the forest canopy provides a refreshing air with minimal pollution.

Labrador Nature Reserve
Locally called Labrador Park, is located in the southern part of mainland Singapore. It is home to the a rocky sea-cliff accessible to the public. The hill is the site of one of the main gun batteries built by the British to defend Singapore. Luscious jungle and paths down to the point.

Visit 'Gardens by The Bay'

Gardens on the bay are a network of modern greenhouses and waterfront parks containing super trees lined with solar cells. Entry to the garden is free, but admission fees apply to the two conservatories: the Flower Dome and Cloud Forest. The gardens offer free tours on Saturday mornings. You can enjoy flora from all over the world here. You won't get phone signal inside. There are beautifully crafted benches all over both domes for you to take in the sights and smells. Bring a book, sit back and relax.

The Singapore orchestra do a lot of shows at Gardens by the Bay, often with quirky themes. There's also a nightly light show: Garden Rhapsody. It happens every day at 7:45 and 8:45. Also check www.sbg.org.sg for times of free concerts staged by Symphony Lake.

 INSIDER HISTORICAL INSIGHT

If you want to splurge try an original Singapore Sling at the near-by historic Raffles Hotel where it was invented (or at least walk around there- it's beautiful).

Pack a picnic and head to the gardens

Even though Singapore's city centre is one of the world's more pleasurable cities to walk around, it's nice to retreat to a quieter place every now and then. When you get an urge to do that, make your way to the city's famous Haw Par Villa. Its a park artfully depicting Chinese history. There are giant statues and dioramas which retell historic Chinese legends and religious mythology.

You must pay a visit to **The Singapore Botanic Gardens;** Singapore's oldest national park is a living, breathing museum of tropical plants. Picnickers, t'ai chi and people practising yoga. The gardens founded in 1859 became a UNESCO World Heritage in 2015 Its free and hosts free tours and seasonal opera performances. Inside the National Orchid Garden charges SG$5 (about $3.75) for adult admission but offers thousands of orchid species, plus bromeliads and carnivorous plants.

INSIDER INSIGHT

BEWARE of Ants and cockroaches. As Singapore is a tropical climate, it's pretty important that you clean up so you don't attract unwanted friends. Don't leave your bags open for them to crawl into!

Visit Singapore's places of worship

Singapore Sultan Mosque

Singapore is home to over 10 religions. Buddhism, Taoism, Islam, Hinduism and Christianity being the most practised. Given this religious diversity its unsurprising that some of Singapore's most fascinating buildings are religious sites. All are free to enter and are definitely well worth a look. Here are the most interesting to pay a visit to:

1. **Thian Hock Keng Temple** (158 Telok Ayer St) is the oldest and most important temple of the Hokkien people. It was built in 1839 for the worship of Mazu, a Chinese sea goddess.
2. **Sri Mariamman Temple** (244 South Bridge Road). Ornate 19th-century Hindu temple Built in 1827, its the oldest Hindu temple in Singapore and features a tower densely ornamented with deities.

3. **Abdul Gafoor Mosque** is an interesting mix of Islamic and Victorian architecture. Completed in 1910, it features an elaborate sundial crowning its main entrance; each of the 25 rays is decorated with Arabic calligraphy denoting the names of 25 prophets. Non-Muslims are asked to refrain from entering the prayer hall at any time, and visitors must dress conservatively.
4. **Sri Veeramakaliamman Temple** - built in 1855 by Tamil labourers, the temple has a South Indian architectural style and a colourful exterior, Its in the middle of Little India and open Sunday to Saturday - 5:00 AM - 9:00 PM
5. **Kong Meng San Phor Kark See Temple** - Singapore's largest (and busiest) Buddhist temple is also an important Vesak Day place of worship. There's also a book shop selling all things Buddhist called the Awareness Place. A canteen that serves purely vegetarian food on special occasions too.
6. **Sultan Mosque** is Singapore's largest mosque, with its striking golden dome, it is a famous landmark in the Malay-dominated Kampung Glam district. The mosque offers free tours. Check here for times: http://sultanmosque.sg/contact-us/visitor-information
7. **St Andrew's Cathedral -** This colonial-era Cathedral was completed in 1862. It's a peaceful location in the centre of Singapore. Its an indelible colonial mark and stands in stark contrast to the nearby skyscrapers.

Visit The Science Centre Singapore

The The Science Centre offers free stargazing every Friday

(weather permitting) between January and November. This is a great free activity and makes for a great educational experience for adults and children. There is limited space, so be sure to arrive by 7:30pm to claim a spot. More details: https://www.science.edu.sg/

Visit Pulau Ubin

Pulau Ubin is an island oasis away from the hustle and bustle of Singapore. Cycle trails and footpaths criss-cross the hills going past traditional kampongs (villages). Bring your own water and snacks as shops are few and far between. It costs $3 by boat from changi point to the island.

Visit Sungei Buloh Wetland Reserve

This wetland is an ASEAN Heritage Park. It was the first wetlands in Singapore to be made into a reserve due to its importance for migratory birds in Asia. There are dozens of bird species but for other wildlife, such as crocodiles, it depends on the season of migration and partly on your luck if you see them at all.

The park is close to the Malaysian boarder, so an excellent stop off if you're continuing on to Malaysia. To get there, board SMRT Bus 925 from Kranji MRT Station. Alight at Kranji Reservoir Carpark B. It costs just S$1.00 to enter.

Explore street art

Colourful murals and graffiti art are displayed throughout Singapore. Murals sometimes cover up entire buildings and symbolize recent and historical events and topics. In Kampong Glam you'll find each street is filled with colourful murals providing an incredible juxtaposition between old and new.

Go Thrift shopping

Thrift and flea market shopping in Singapore is a great experience, with many of its wealthy inhabitants casting away their unwanted designer wares. Check out New2U Thrift Shop and Praisehaven Mega Family Thrift first for bargain pieces. If you don't find any treasures there Google for the most expensive area in Singapore (at the time of writing Orchard). Then put second hand shop or the American term Thrift store into Google Maps. Start with the most expensive areas and work your way through until the middle-tier ones. You will be really surprised by what you find.

Explore the best markets

Singapores markets are a fun and eye-opening plunge into local culture and, unless you succumb to the persistent vendors, it will cost you nothing.

Chinatown was founded in 1966, and is a bastion of bargains from morning until night. Go early in the morning and then come back at night for two totally different experiences. Make sure to barter with all sales people. The vendors always offer the lowest price always when you walk away.

Sungei Road Thieve's Market is an interesting air conditioned Sunday flea market focusing on vintage keepsakes like Chinese ceramics.

Bugis Street is the biggest street shopping location in Singapore. The place itself is rundown and the layout is very confusing. If you have patience you can pick up some good buys here.

Telok Ayer Market, officially called Lau Pa Sat. The market is one of the biggest hawker centres in Singapore. Go to the places where you see lot of locals and you won't be disappointed by anything you eat. The pepper crab and Satay will undoubtably wow your taste buds.

The **Tekka Centre** is market with mostly Indian vendors selling everything imaginable. There's a great hawker stand attached with an amazing variety of foods. It is very atmospheric and the prices are low.

Go to the Movies on the cheap

Go to Shaw, WE Cinema or Filmgarde cinemas on Tuesdays to get up to 50% off the ticket price. Singaporeans love to watch movies and, at around S$12.50 per ticket, it's great value. You can enjoy a movie at VivoCity, the largest cinema in Singapore for just $5 from Monday to Wednesday. Singapore's cinemas crank up the air conditioning, so wear something warm.

INSIDER MONEY SAVING INSIGHT

MovieMob specialises in screening drive-in films across different venues in Singapore. Most of the outdoor movies are held in the Marina Bay Sands Event Square. Check MovieMob for the latest schedule.

The best cheap massage

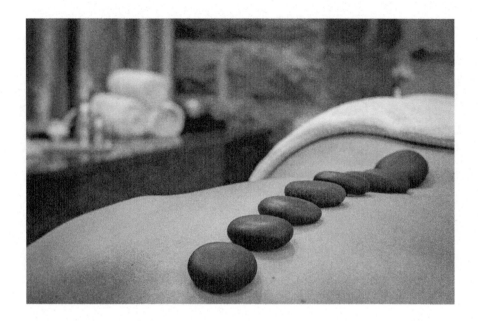

Travelling can be stressful. A good massage calms the nervous system and relieves tension. The best bang for your buck massage in Singapore is without doubt Healing Touch spas. Prices start at $20 for an hours massage: https://www.healingtouchspa.-com/. Sabaai Sabaai offers the best Thai massage in Singapore, and prices start at $30 USD.

Explore the most interesting neighbourhoods

Singapore is a patchwork of different neighbours. These are the nicest places to stroll around when you need a day off from the cities chaos:

Holland Village is the most upscale part of Singapore but it attracts mostly expats. The area around Botanic Gardens commands the highest real estate prices.

Tiong Bahru makes for a lovely afternoon. It's an enchanting blend of traditional and new, lined with funky coffee shops and cute shops.

Keong Saik is a super-trendy but super-expensive Singapore hotspot but a walk will cost you nothing.

 INSIDER LOCAL INSIGHT

Singapore doesn't have any unsafe areas, but Yishin and Punggol are considered bad because poorer people reside there. As mentioned, Geylang is associated with prostitution and migrant workers, but it is also one of the cheapest parts of Singapore and quite safe.

Escape the crowds

Helix Bridge

Singapore is an overcrowded island home to 5.6 million, theres no escaping it. If you are easily overwhelmed by crowds visit the obvious attractions as early as possible, peak people flow is 11 am to 5 pm so get up early to enjoy the attractions serenely. Luckily Singapore also has many hidden gems that aren't commercialised or too crowded most of the time. Here are the best:

- The library at The Esplanade makes for a perfect retreat. No one ever goes there even though its right smack in the middle of the city. Inside theres a corner with big windows and great skyline views.
- Changi Beach village makes for a perfect restful weekend afternoon. The vibe is relaxed and theres a nice sea breeze. Planes land very nearby so it will feel as if some are almost on top of you.

- Walk from Lavender to Geylang after 10 pm - The whole stretch is quiet and very pleasant to walk.
- Japanese Cemetery Park - A place to meditate whilst paying your respects to the departed. Its also an excellent location for photography..
- Bay East Garden - This is a really good photography spot of the major landmarks of Singapore. The area is safe even at night.
- Henderson Waves - This bridge is high above sea level. It has a great view of the southern part of Singapore and has some seating places on the bridge. It's a great stopover for those trekking along Mount Faber Park.
- Bedok Reservoir Park - Absolutely the best place to Relax and Workout. There is an adventure Activity area also attached at the Pool side.
- SuperTree by IndoChine has the best rooftop view in the whole city.
- Helix Bridge - this steel footbridge was opened in 2010, inspired by the curved form of the structure of DNA. The view of Marina Bay Sands is breathtaking at night.
- If crowds are really not your thing the best solution is to become a night owl while in Singapore.

Watch Free Live Music

Singapore features an ever-changing number of clubs, bars and live music. Here are the places to head to for some cheap drinks and free live music. You'll find everything from Jazz to Irish folk music:

- Live music bar Singapore · In Clarke Quay this purposively ruinous bar has graffiti-covered walls and a casual vibe with regular free live music.
- Blu Jaz Cafe - One of the best cafes in Arab street area. Reasonable price, great food, a lot of cuisines. Outdoor seating with live music every night.
- Cafe Singapore · Near the Sultan temple they offer international eats and live bands.
- Wala Wala Cafe Singapore is a laid-back beer and eats place with live bands nightly.
- Crazy Elephant is a touristy place but with excellent Happy hours (5pm to 9pm) and a variety of interesting musical acts which start at 9pm.

Drink promotions to look out for

Singapore is an expensive city to drink in. A beer at most city bars will set you back between S$10 and S$18. At the Hawker centres you'll pay between $3 and S$7 for bottles of Tiger. To get around this indulge in three common drinks promotions: free-flow, liquid buffet and ladies nights (if you're female, of course!)

Idle at Prinsep offers the cheapest drinks promotions in the city. From 5-11pm on Thursdays, ladies get free-flow gin, vodka, rum, bourbon, whisky or beer for S$9.90. Guys pay $25. Go early to avoid the crowds.

If you're female go to some ladies nights to save youself money.

80 of 178

Club street (near Somerset MRT station) has many bars with pretty good steals during happy hour (5-7pm). Men can cut costs by buying beer from supermarket. It's legal to drink in public in Singapore but only from 10.30pm to 7am.

💡 INSIDER MONEY SAVING TIP

Watch Free comedy at The Merry Lion Comedy Cafe And Bar on Monday nights when the comedy show is free and save yourself $15. Address: Circular Rd, #03-00 8b.

Not super cheap, but loved

Combine the Singapore Zoo and Night Safari

The Singapore Zoo is an open-air zoo with over 270 animals. Animals aren't locked up in tiny cages. They offer a night tour in a different section of the park where you get to see the nocturnal animals. If you combine the day and night tickets together, you'll save a lot of money. Admission to the zoo is 35 SGD for adults and 23 SGD for kids. The night safari is 47 SGD for adults and 31 SGD for kids. A combination ticket for the zoo and night safari is 68 SGD for adults and 48 SGD for kids. If you book online you also get 15% off the ticket: https://www.wrs.com.sg/en/singapore-zoo/visit.html

Go to one of the pick-up points on Orchard Road for the shuttle bus to the Night Safari.

Visit Jurong Bird Park

The Jurong Bird Park is home to 400 bird species from parrots to penguins. You'll see birds from all over the world. There are a variety of vulture shows and penguins shows. The public can also feed the birds and penguins. Kids are particularly fond of this park. An adult ticket costs $25 for an and a child's ticket costs $16.

Do a Brewery tour

Singapore is home to lots of delicious craft breweries. The Tiger Brewery offers tours for S$18. Tours must be booked in advance and run every hour and include beer tasting. https://tigerbrewery-tour.com.sg/

Visit the last traditional craftsmen of Singapore

Due to high-tech machines traditional crafts are disappearing in Singapore. You can see and speak to the last master craftsmen through the **Disappearing Trades Tour**, a guided tour that allows you to listen to their stories and see them at work. Its expensive and starts at sgd$98

Don't leave Singapore without seeing (even if only from outside)

Universal Studios Singapore
Movie amusement park with sets & rides on themes from Hollywood to sci-fi, plus live entertainment. Prices start at $79 for a one day adult pass to $108 for an adult season pass.

Merlion Park
Iconic, 8.5m-tall statue with the body of a fish & head of a lion, shooting water from its mouth.

Clarke Quay
Mall with restaurants & nightlife in redeveloped, 19th-century, riverside commercial district.

East Coast Park
White, sandy beach with a skate park, water sports and sports facilities, plus local food sellers.

VivoCity
Expansive, modern shopping center hosting a wide range of retailers, restaurants & theaters.

Fort Canning Hill
Historical hilltop site with events
A well-known historical landmark, this grassy hilltop park hosts events such as concerts & plays.

Tiger Sky Tower

131m ascent for panoramic views. An enclosed cabin ro-
tates to the top of this high observation tower with sweeping
views.

Wings Of Time
Modern venue featuring a nightly show with colorful lights,
lasers, water fountains & 3D effects.

Fountain of Wealth
Huge contemporary outdoor fountain in a shopping complex, offering nightly light shows.

Singapore Food and drink hacks

You don't have to spend a lot to eat the most incredible memory forming meals in Singapore.

Eat at Hawker Centres

Hawker centres are open-air complexes selling cheap food. Eat at them and you could spend as little as $10 a day for three meals.

Hawker Centre Manners

- Bag a seat first; it's normal to share with strangers.
- If there's a table number, note it as the stall owner uses it as a reference for food delivery.

- If the stall has a 'self service' sign, you'll have to carry the food to the table yourself. Otherwise, the vendor brings your order to you.
- Ignore wandering touts who try to sit you down and plonk menus in front of you.
- return your tray once finished, although there are a few roaming cleaners who'll take your empty dishes.

💡 INSIDER LOCAL INSIGHT

Locals often *chope* 'reserve' seats at a hawker centre using packets of tissue paper. So if you see tissues on a seat, its taken.

Eat Street food

A visit to Singapore without eating from street vendors would be unthinkable. You can eat for under a dollar from street vendors. Some worry about eating street food, but as long as you follow where the locals are queuing you'll never have any problems.

Go to kopitiams

Coffeeshops, also called kopitiams are open shopfront cafes, usually with a handful of stalls and roaming 'aunties' or 'uncles' taking drinks orders. Heap Seng Leong will take you back to the 1980's and is super cheap.

Free coffee refills

Save a little cash while *still* feeding your caffeine habit, you can get free refills at Starbucks. They offer free refills on filtered coffee and teas, great if you need a laptop day.

Best bang for your buck all-you-can-eat

All you can eat buffets are a great way to stock on on nutritious food while travelling. Dishes like fish are normally expensive, but at Kiseki Japanese Buffet Restaurant you can chow down on your omega 3's for much less. There lunch menu is just S$15. Don't drink much water or eat bread and you'll get more than your money's worth.

Find deals to eat out
Great sites to visit include Hungry Deals, Yelp Deals, Groupon, LivingSocial, and Valpak.

Free food
If you're really hard up you can go to for free food at Sri Krishna Mandir ,Singapore. For ethical reasons I would only go here, if you're really struggling, and if you are, I'm sorry, that sucks. Make sure to check out our section on finding work while travelling. Things like teaching English online are easy to get started.

Must-try Street Food

Singapore is home to some of the World's best street food. Follow the locals, if local people are waiting you know it's going to be tasty. These are my favourite dishes in Singapore:

- Bak Kut Teh (肉骨茶 lit.Meat Bone Tea/ Pork Ribs Soup)
- Wanton Mee (云吞面)
- Fried Carrot Cake (菜头粿) No, this isn't the Western dessert.
- Dim Sum (点心)
- Kaya Toast & Soft-Boiled Eggs.

- Frog porridge. Don't be put off by the name. Its actually really tasty.
- Hainanese chicken rice.
- Red snapper head curry.
- Curry laksa
- Zhajiangmian (beef noodles).

💡 INSIDER LOCAL INSIGHT

Singaporeans refer to strangers such as street food and hawker centre stall owners as "Aunties" and "Uncles". This is an endearing way of addressing people, but only for those over 60. Be careful using this term, it can cause offence among younger people.

Cheap Eats

It's actually quite hard to have a bad meal in Singapore, but it's easy to have an overpriced one. Fill your stomach without emptying your wallet by trying these local restaurants all with mains under $8.

Note: Download the offline map for Singapore on Google maps, (instructions 1. go to app 2. select offline apps in the left sidebar 3. go to the area you want to download 4. click download). Then simply type the restaurant names in to navigate, add the restaurants to your favourites by clicking the star icon so you can see where the cheap eats are when you're out and about to avoid wasting your money at hyped tourist joints)

Sungei Road Laksa
Hawker Stall
Blk 27 Jalan Berseh #01-100
The best laksa's in Singapore.

Kim Dae Mun Korean Food
100 Orchard Road, #01-03
The Korean food here is amazing and really cheap.

Thai Gold Food
91 Bencoolen St, #01-14/22, Sunshine Plaza
Simple but delicious Thai food at really low prices.

Zhong Guo La Mian Xiao Long Bao
Hawker Stall
#02-135, 335 Smith St
Food is good and cheap. Try their Xiao Long Bao, a Chinese steamed bun, you won't be disappointed.

BK Eating House

Coffee Shop
21 South Bridge Rd Singapore
Cheap and tasty food and beers in the middle of CBD. A rare find.

Little Hiro
559 Bukit Timah Rd
Cheap delicious Hawaiian food.

Steakout Singapore
89 Victoria St
Very affordable and tasty steaks.

Ayam Penyet Ria
204 Orchard Road, #04-25/26 & level 1, Lucky Plaza
Easygoing Indonesian offering smashed fried chicken.

Chinatown Food Street
Hawker Centre on Smith St
Always a great place to go for cheap beers and tasty food.

Swee Choon Tim Sum Restaurant
Jln Besar, 183-191
Very cheap dim sum and high quality.

La Petite Cuisine
10 Jalan Serene
Cheap French food.

Tian Tian Hainanese Chicken Rice
Hawker Stall
1 Kadayanallur St, #01 -10/11 Maxwell Food Center
Delicious and cheap chicken dishes.

Saveur
14 Scotts Road, #01-07B Far East Plaza
Cheap French food; comparable to upscale restaurants.

iSTEAKS
1 Maju Avenue, #02-03/04/05/06 , myVillage
Great steak house food at cheap prices.

Thai Tantric Authentic Thai Cuisine
400 Orchard Road, #03-44 Orchard Towers
Very good Thai food and cheap price.

Is the tap water drinkable?

Yes. Unlike other countries in Southeast Asia, the tap water in Singapore is safe to drink. A bottle of water costs S$2 at mini-marts so refill to save.

How much can you save haggling here?

Singapore is no Bangkok, but you can still haggle. You can save a lot by haggling at markets. Start low and work your way up with humour. When you walk away, the person you're haggling with, will call you back, and this is when you will get the lowest price.

Need to Know before you go

Currency: Singapore dollar

Languages: English, Tamil Malay Mandarin Chinese Standard Mandarin

Money: Widely available ATMs.

Visas: check http://www.doyouneedvisa.com/

Time: GMT + 8

When to Go

High Season: July and August.

Shoulder: May, April, June

Low Season: September to May.

Important Numbers

911

Watch to understand the History

Singapore 's history is fascinating. There are tons of documentaries. City of the Future: Singapore – Full Episode | National Geographic is a great one to watch before your visit. Just type it into YouTube to watch.

Basic Phrases

Here are some Practical Malay phrases that are easy to remember to help you save money, make friends and avoid annoying the locals. Please repeat after the speaker.

Hello	Helo
Yes	Ya
No	Tidak
How much?	Berapa banyak?
Discount?	Diskaun?
I am on a budget	Saya ada anggaran
I am from _____	Saya berasal dari _____
My name is	Nama saya ialah
How to I find the train / metro / bus?	Bagaimana untuk mencari kereta api / metro / bas?
I would like a beer, please.	Saya mahu bir.
Where is the bathroom?	Di manakah bilik air?
Can you show me on this map?	Bolehkah anda menunjukkan saya di peta ini?
Where is _____?	Di manakah _____?
I'm lost.	Saya tersesat.
Do you speak English?	Adakah anda berbahasa Inggeris?
Can you speak slower?	Bolehkah anda bercakap lebih perlahan?
Do you have WIFI?	Adakah anda mempunyai WIFI?
What is the WIFI password?	Apakah kata laluan WIFI?
Sorry	Maaf
Thank you	Terima kasih
Goodbye	Selamat tinggal
Please	Tolonglah
Good Evening	Selamat petang

Getting Out of Singapore cheaply

Bus

Red Bus are the cheapest bus operator with tickets to Kuala Lumpur for just $8. Booking ahead can save you up to 70% of the cost of the ticket. redbus.sg

Plane

At the time of writing Jetstar and Air Asia are the cheapest carrier with onward flights from Singapore. Take advantage

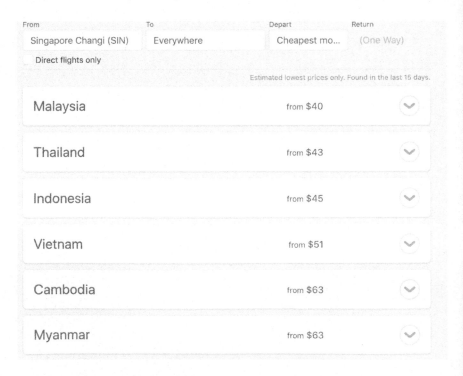

of discounts and specials. Sign up for e-newsletters from

local carriers including Jetstar, Air Asia and Scoot to learn about special fares. Be careful with cheap airlines, most will allow **hand-luggage only**, and some charge for anything that is not a backpack. Check their websites before booking if you need to take luggage.

Avoid these tourist traps or scams

Singapore is a very safe city. Like anywhere there are pickpockets lurking around attractions and crowded areas. Don't keep things in your back pockets or wear a bag that can be easily opened. Thieves are opportunistic thieves rather than forceful. There are three common scams in Singapore. Here's how to avoid them:

1. Stick to Grab (taxi app). It is not uncommon for Taxi Drivers to drive the Long Way - to charge you more, much more!

2. Check your bill before you pay. Overcharging tourists is common in local eateries.

3. Fake Electronics are a problem, don't buy these at market-type setups.

Fully costed breakdown

	How	Cost normally / advice	Cost when following suggested tip
How I got from the airport to the city	MRT	$45 Taxi	$3.50
Where I stayed	Hostel in the city centre for $15 with free breakfast	Hotels are upwards of $120 a night unless hacked.	$45
Tastiest street foods I ate and cost	Fried Carrot Cake (菜头粿)	You don't have to spend a fortune to eat well in Singapore.	$3 average
How I got around	Walked and cycled and used the MRT.	The cities relatively flat, so try cycling to keep costs low. The MRT 2 day card is $16 so fit all the tourist attractions in then.	$16
What I saw and paid	Beaches, free museums, free tours, hikes, treetop walks, temples and traditional villages	You don't need to go to all the expensive attractions in Singapore to have a ball here.	$10
My onward flight	Bangkok $9 with Air Asia	Book six weeks ahead for the lowest price.	$9
My Total costs	US$150		$150

RECAP: How to have a $1,000 trip to Singapore on a $150 budget

Five star hotels

Book Last minute 5 star hotels. Check on the same day of your stay for cheap five star hotel cheap deals. Go to booking.com enter Singapore, tonight, only one night and filter by 5 stars. This can be very effective on the weekends in the low season (July and August) when hotels empty of their business travellers. Potential saving $800.

Take advantage of street eats and Hawker centres

Street food and hawker centres can save you hundreds on eating in Singapore. Remember to go where the locals are eating. Potential saving $200.

Go to museums/ attractions on their free days

The average traveller spends $180 on museums in Singapore, but there's an abundance of free or cheap attractions that are just as amazing. Potential saving $180.

Do all the free stuff first

The natural environment in Singapore is an endless bounty of interesting and inspiring things to experience and wildlife to spot. Start free and be mindful of what you want to pay for. Potential savings: $200.

Book Ahead

Book six weeks ahead for the lowest prices on outward buses and flights. Potential savings: $150

PRACTICAL THINGS TO REMEMBER TO SAVE MONEY IN SINGAPORE

- Download google maps for for use offline
- Download the Malay language pack on google translate - you will be grateful you have it if you want to talk to older Singaporeans.
- Bring a good mosquito spray or combine a few drops of lemongrass oil with a moisturiser and rub if everywhere especially for tree-top and nature walks. This is the technique the Inca's used to keep mosquitos at bay. The smell turns the mosquitos away from your skin. Mosquitos can be a big nuisance here.
- Know the names of street foods to try and the places to try them.
- Plan to start sightseeing early for a more serene experience.
- Book your accommodation ahead of time if visiting for the Singapore Grand Prix - prices skyrocket.
- Don't eat at any restaurants with touts outside.
- Don't eat near famous attractions, go around the corner for much lower prices.
- Star the best Hawker centres to eat at on Google maps: Tiong Bahru Food Centre. Lau Pa Sat. Changi Village Hawker Centre. Amoy Street Food Centre, and Chomp Chomp Food Centre.
- Pack a travel snorkel kit if you want to snorkel on Sentosa or Pulau. Its a great free activity when you have your own equipment. And you can easily fold down a travel snorkel to fit in hand luggage.
- Avoid over-scheduling. You don't want to pack so much into your trip you wind up feeling like you're working on the conveyor belt called best sights of Singapore instead of fully saturating your senses in the incredible sights, sounds, smells of Singapore.

- Pack food for the airport, you'll save $10 on a bad cup of coffee and stale croissant.

The secret to saving HUGE amounts of money when travelling to Singapore is...

Your mindset. Money is an emotional topic, if you associate words like cheapskate with being thrifty when travelling you are likely to say 'F-it' and spend your money needlessly because you associate pain with saving money. You pay now for an immediate reward. Our brains are prehistoric; they focus on surviving day to day. Travel companies and hotels know this and put trillions into making you believe you will be happier when you spend on their products or services. Our poor brains are up against outdated programming and an onslaught of advertisements bombarding us with the message: spending money on travel equals PLEASURE. To correct this carefully lodged propaganda in your frontal cortex you need to imagine your future self.

Saving money does not make you a cheapskate. It makes you smart. How do people get rich? They invest their money. They don't go out and earn it; they let their money earn more money. So every time you want to spend money, imagine this: while you travel your money is working for you, not you for money. While you sleep the money you've invested is going up and up. That's a pleasure a pricey entrance fee can't give you. Thinking about putting your money to work for you tricks your brain into believing you are not withholding pleasure from yourself, you are saving your money to invest so you can go to even more amazing places. You are thus turning thrifty travel into a pleasure fueled sport.

When you've got money invested - If you want to splash your cash on a first-class airplane seat - you can. I can't tell you how to invest your money, only that you should. Saving $20 on taxi's doesn't seem like much but over time you could be saving upwards of $15,000 a year, which is a deposit for a house which you can rent on Airbnb to finance more travel. Your brain making money looks like your brain on cocaine, so tell yourself saving money is making money.

Scientists have proved that imagining your future self is the easiest way to associate pleasure with saving money. You can download FaceApp — which will give you a picture of what you will look like older and greyer, or you can take a deep breath just before spending money and ask yourself if you will regret the purchase later.

The easiest ways to waste money travelling are:

Getting a taxi. The solution to this is to always download the google map before you go. Many taxi drivers will drive you around for 15 minutes when the place you were trying to get to is a 5-minute walk… remember while not getting an overpriced taxi to tell yourself, 'I am saving money to free myself for more travel.'
Spending money on overpriced food when hungry. The solution: carry snacks. A banana and an apple will cost you, in most places less than a dollar.
Spending on entrance fees to top-rated attractions. If you really want to do it, spend the money happily. If you're conflicted sleep on it. I don't regret spending $200 on a skydive over the Great Barrier Reef, I do regret going to the top of the shard in London for $60. Only you can know but make sure it's your decision and not the marketing directors at said top-rated attraction.
Telling yourself 'you only have the chance to see/eat/experience it now'. While this might be true, make sure YOU WANT to spend the money. Money spent is money you can't invest, and often you can have the same experience for much less.

You can experience luxurious travel on a small budget which will trick your brain into thinking you're already a high-roller, which will mean you'll be more likely to start acting like one and invest your money. Stay in five-star hotels for $5 by booking on the day of your stay on booking.com to enjoy last minute deals. You can go to fancy restaurants using daily deal sites. Ask your airline about last minute upgrades to first-class or business. I paid $100 extra on a $179 ticket to Cuba from Germany to be bumped to Business Class. When you ask you will be surprised what you can get both at hotels and airlines.

Travel, as the saying goes is the only thing you spend money on that makes you richer. In practice, you can easily waste money, making it difficult to enjoy that metaphysical wealth. The biggest money saving secret is to turn bargain hunting into a pleasurable activity, not an annoyance. Budgeting consciously can be fun, don't feel disappointed because you don't spend the $60 to go into an attraction, feel good because soon that $60 will soon be earning money for you. Meaning, you'll have the time and money to enjoy more metaphysical wealth, while your bank balance increases.

Enjoy your first Day for under $20

Start your day by taking in a bird's eye view of Singapore by walking from Vivocity along the Sentosa Boardwalk that connects to Sentosa. When you arrive do the nature walk in Sentosa. Upon returning to the mainland, enjoy the air conditioning in Vivo City shopping mall before taking the metro bound for Chinatown. Explore the streets around Chinatown. Treat yourself to a bargain pair of shades or shorts before sitting down to some lunch at one of the restaurants on Trengganu Street. Visit Sri Mariamman Temple on South Bridge Road, one of the city's most fascinating buildings. Visit 'Esplanades - Theatres on the Bay' for some great photos. Explore Singapore's most vibrant neighbourhood, Little India. When you get back finish the night off in one of the many bars on Boat Quay, Clarke Quay, or the karaoke-bar central on Circular Road.

So there it is, you can save a small fortune in Singapore by being strategic with your trip planning. We've arranged everything in the guide to offer the best bang for your buck. Which means we took the view that if it's not a good investment for your money, we wouldn't include it. Why would a guide called 'Super Cheap Singapore' include lots of overpriced attractions? That said if you think we've missed something or have unanswered questions ping me an email philgtang@gmail.com .I'm on central Europe time and usually reply within 8 hours of getting your mail.

Don't put your dreams off!

Time is a currency you never get back and travel is its greatest return on investment. Plus now you know you can visit Singapore for a fraction of the price most would have you believe. Go to Singapore and create unforgettable memories - on the cheap!

Websites to save you Money

1. **TalkTalkbnb.com** - Here you stay for free when you teach the host your native language
2. Rome2Rio.com - the go to site for good travel prices on train, bus, planes etc. Especially good for paths less travelled.
3. couchsurfing.com - stay for free with a local - always check reviews.
4. trustedhousesitter.com - always check reviews
5. booking.com - now sends you vouchers for discounts in the city when you book through them
6. blablacar.com - travel in car with locals already going to your destination
7. airbnb.com for both accommodation and experiences.
8. hostelbookers.com - book hostels
9. https://www.greatdeals.com.sg - deals in Singapore
10. Download Klook app for discounted tickets in Singapore
11. Traveloka for discounted hotels.

Thank you for reading

Dear Lovely Reader,

If you have found this book useful, please consider writing a short review on Amazon.

One person from every 1000 readers leaves a review on Amazon. It would mean more than you could ever know if you were one of our 1 in 1000 people to take the time to write a short review.

We are a group of four friends who all met travelling 15 years ago. We believe that great experiences don't need to blow your budget, just your mind.

Thank you so much for reading again and for spending your time and investing your trips future in Super Cheap Insider Guides.

One last note, please don't listen to anyone who says 'Oh no, you can't visit Singapore on a budget'. Unlike you they didn't have this book. The truth is you can do ANYWHERE on a budget with the right insider advice and planning. Sure, learning to travel to Singapore on a budget that doesn't compromise on anything or drastically compromise on safety or comfort levels is a skill, but this guide has done the detective work for you. Now it is time for you to put the advice into action.

Phil

P.S If you need any more super cheap tips we'd love to hear from you e-mail me at philgtang@gmail.com, we have a lot of contacts in every region, so if there's a specific bargain you're hunting we can help you find it :-)

SHOP 150 VACATIONS UNDER $150.

INCLUDING LONDON.

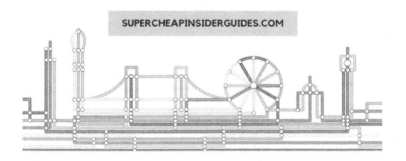

UNCOVERED A SUPER CHEAP TIP DURING
YOUR TRAVELS? GET PAID FOR IT.
EMAIL PHILGTANG@GMAIL.COM

WE PAY
FOR TIPS

CHOOSE FROM PRO RATA
ROYALTIES OR A $50 AMAZON
VOUCHER

Bonus Budget Travel Hacks

I've included these bonus travel hacks to help you plan and enjoy your trip to Singapore cheaply, joyfully and smoothly. Perhaps they will even inspire you or renew your passion for long-term travel.

From saving space in your pack to scoring cheap flights, there are a wealth of generic travel hacks to help you enjoy stress-free, happier travels without breaking the bank. This is why I've included this bonus section to maximise the value you get from buying this book.

When I tell people I write a travel guide series focused on luxurious budget travel, they wrongly assume that's impossible and often say 'Hitchhiking and couch-surfing?'. Others with more vivid imaginations ask me if I recommend hooking up with older men or women... Of course, they are surprised when I tell them that not one of the 150 Super Cheap Guides endorses such practises because they maximise discomfort. They look at me dumbfounded and ask 'How on earth do you travel comfortably on a budget then?'

Travelling cheaply in a way that doesn't compromise enjoyment, comfort or safety is a skill I have honed over 20 years of travelling. My foremost learning was that locals always know the tricks and tips to enjoy the same or a better tourist experience for a 10th of the cost, and that's why I teamed up with locals in each locale to distil the tips that will save you a fortune without compromising on enjoyment or comfort.

Enjoyable budget travel is about balancing and prioritising what is important to you.
When I tell people about my methodology I often receive long defensive monologues about why they spend so much on travel, or why they can't or don't travel. Thats why we will first discuss how you can find the freedom to travel.

How to find the free-dom to travel

Freedom is one of those words that can mean different things to different people. It's important to be clear on what it looks like to you in your life, and all the stories and beliefs that prevent you from having it. For me, freedom means always having at choice in my life. I don't do anything that I don't want to do. —LEO BABAUTA

We've spoken a lot about how to save money travelling to Singapore, but how do you find the freedom if you have:

1. Pets
2. Kids
3. A spouse who doesn't want you to travel
4. A job that keeps you at home?

Like everything, there's a solution to every problem. In this chapter, I want to you to think about whether your excuses can be overcome using the following solutions, because as Randy Komisar said: "And then there is the most dangerous risk of all – the risk of spending your life not doing what you want on the bet you can buy yourself the freedom to do it later."

Pets

I have a dog, an extremely loving German Shepherd. And when I travel overland from Austria she comes with me and my wife. If we are heading on a longer trip we either leave her with friends or family or we get someone to house sit for us. housesitters.-com offers up people who are vetted and reviewed and in exchange for free accommodation will care for your pets. Just be aware it often works out financially better to rent your space on Airbnb and pay someone to look after your pets. Make sure you visit their facilities before you entrust your pet to anyone and of course, always read the reviews.

I know a lot of people miss their pets travelling which is why we endeavour to take our dog with us. Exploring with her has formed some of our most precious memories. If you're flying with your pet always look up the rules and make sure you comply. If you're going to the UK for example, they quarantine dogs who come in by air. So we only take our dog by car. Coming into the UK by car, dogs must need to be chipped, have a note from a vet saying they are clear of Rabies and tapeworms, have a pet passport and be on a course of medication for tapeworms 2 days before they enter. The UK is the strictest country I've encountered when it comes to travelling with pets so I use this as barometer. My point is, do your homework if you're bringing your furry friend, both about entry conditions and the local environment for your pet. For instance, in India, many domesticated dogs are attacked by street dogs. Educate yourself on your options and limitations but don't think because you have pets that travel is out of the question.

Kids

I also have a daughter who is about to turn 1. We have travelled to seven countries with her so far, with many more in the pipeline. The easiest way to travel with kids is in an RV. You don't have to worry about checking vast amounts of baggage or travelling with a stroller. You have unlimited freedom and can camp for free in many places. You can normally take the RV on a slow ship cheaper than the price of a plane ticket for 3 people.

A study by Cornell University found that we get more happiness from anticipating a travel experience in comparison to anticipating buying a new possession, so in that way, money can buy you happiness. If you invest in an RV, you can also turn it into a profit centre by renting it out on platforms like www.outdoorsy.com.

You don't necessarily have to fly to travel with kids, train, bus and RV's are better options. Kids become more adaptable and flexible when the world is their classroom. This is true at any age. but when kids immerse themselves in new places and engage with local cultures; this open-mindedness helps them in all aspects of their lives. For school-age children, you are limited to

119 of 178

holiday dates, but with 12 weeks off a year, you can still find adventure together.

A spouse who doesn't want you to travel

A loving partner should always want what's best for you. Scientifically, travelling is proven to reduce stress. A study in 2000 study found that men and women who do not take a trip for several years are 30 per cent more likely to have a heart attack. It makes sense because when you travel you are more active; travellers often walk ten miles a day, sightseeing and soaking up new sights and smells.

Travelling also strengthens the 'openness' aspect of your personality and makes you less emotionally reactive to day-to-day changes, improving emotional stability. Sure, losing your baggage or almost missing a connecting flight can be panic-inducing, but, overall, the data supports that travelling is beneficial for you. Tell your partner about these studies, if they don't want a healthier, happier, more emotionally stable you, then it may be time to consider why you're investing your time with this person.

Another common issue is mismatched travel budgets. If you and your partner travel together and they force you to overspend with the 'we're on holiday/vacation!' appendage, here's a tip from one of our writers Kim:

'My husband and I were always having 'discussions' about money during our trips. I love bargains and he is the kind of traveller who's totally cool to be ripped off because he normally travels for business and has become used to spending corporate money. The compromise we reached is that he reads a shoestring or super cheap guide before the trip. Then when he wants to waste money, I say yes, but only in exchange for doing one budget item from the guide. It has worked wonders, lessened our 'discussions' and he now actually chooses cheaper destinations as he sees budgeting as a game.'

A job that keeps you at home

Our lives can feel constantly busy. Sometimes we may feel we are sinking beneath our workload. If you're close to or suffering a burnout the stress relief that comes from novelty and change in the form of new people, sights and experiences is the best remedy you could give to yourself.

If you're in a job that is hurting your health or well-being its time to reconsider why. It is often the case that you believe the work to be deeply rewarding, but if that reward leaves you ill, uninspired and fatigued, you can't help anyone. I learnt this the hard way when I worked for a charity whose mission I deeply resonated with. After 3 years of 70 hour work weeks, I'd lost hair, teeth, direction and, if I'm honest, faith in humanity. It took me 3 years to come back to the light and see that I chose a very stressful job that my body told me repeatedly it could not handle. Travel was a big part of forgiving myself. It helped me put old stories that held me back and probably sent me into this quagmire of self-abuse via work into perspective.

Sometimes we keep letting ourselves make excuses about why we're not travelling because we're scared of the unknown. In such cases, one of three things happens that forces a person from their nest:

- A traumatic event
- Completing a major milestone
- A sudden realisation or epiphany

Do yourself a favour, don't wait for any of those. Decide you want to travel, and book a flight. Our next section takes you through how to book the cheapest possible flight.

HOW TO FIND CHEAP FLIGHTS

"The use of travelling is to regulate imagination by reality, and instead of thinking how things may be, to see them as they are." S amuel Jackson

If you're working full-time you can save yourself a lot of money

by requesting your time off from work starting in the middle of the week. Tuesdays and Wednesdays are the cheapest days to fly, you can save hundreds just by adjusting your time off.

The simplest secret to booking cheap flights is open parameters. Let's say you want to fly from Chicago to Paris. You

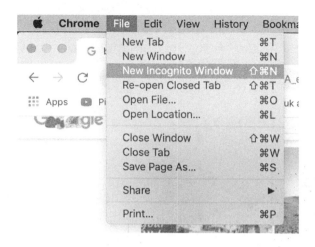

need to enter USA to France, you may find flights from NYC to Paris for $70 and can take a cheap flight to NYC. Make sure you calculate full costs, including if you need airport accommodation and of course getting to and from airports, but in every instance open parameters will save you at least half the cost of the flight.

If you're not sure about where you want to go, use open parameters to show you the cheapest destinations from your city.
Use skyscanner.net - they include the low-cost airlines that others like Kayak leave out.

Open parameters can also show you the cheapest dates to fly. If you're flexible you can save up to 80% of the flight cost. Always check the weather at your destination before you book, sometimes a $400 flight will be $20, because its monsoon season. But hey, if you like the rain, why not?

ALWAYS USE A PRIVATE BROWSER TO BOOK FLIGHTS

Skyscanner and other sites track your IP address and put prices up and down based on what they determine your strength of conviction to buy. e.g if you've booked one-way and are looking for the return these sites will jack the prices up by in most cases 50%. Incognito browsing pays.

Use a VPN such as Hola to book your flight from your destination

Install Hola, change your destination to the country you are flying to. The location from which a ticket is booked can affect the price significantly as algorithms take into account local buying power.

Choose the right time to buy your ticket.

Choose the right time to buy your ticket, as purchasing tickets on a Sunday has been proven to be cheaper. If you can only book during the week, try to do it on a Tuesday.

Mistake fares

Email alerts from individual carriers are where you can find the best 'mistake fares". This is where a computer error has resulted in an airline offering the wrong fare. In my experience its best to sign up to individual carriers email lists but if you ARE lazy Secret Flying puts together a daily roster of mistake fares. Visit   to see if there's any errors that can benefit you.

Fly late for cheaper prices.

Red-eye flights, the ones that leave later in the day, are typically cheaper and less crowded, so aim to book that flight if possible. You will also get through the airport much quicker at the end of the day, just make sure there's ground transport available for when you land. You don't want to save $50 on the airfare and spend it on a taxi to your accommodation.

Use this APP for same day flights

If you're plans are flexible, use 'Get The Flight Out' (
) a fare tracker Hopper that shows you
same-day deeply discounted flights. This is best for long-
haul flights with major carriers. You can often find a British
Airways round-trip from JFK Airport to Heathrow for $300. If
you booked this in advance you'd pay at least double.

Take an empty water bottle with you

Airport prices on food and drinks are sky-high. It disgusts
me to see some airports charging $10 for a bottle of water.
ALWAYS take an empty water bottle with you. It's relatively
unknown, but most airports have drinking water fountains
past the security check. Just type in your airport name to
                              to locate the fountain. Then once
you've passed security (because they don't allow you to
take 100ml or more of liquids) you can freely refill your bottle with water.

Round-the-World (RTW) Tickets

It is always cheaper to book your flights using a DIY approach.
First, you may decide you want to stay longer in one country,
and a RTW will charge you a hefty fee for changing your flight.
Secondly, it all depends on where and when you travel and as
we have discussed, there are many ways to ensure you pay way
less than $1,500 for a year of flights. If you're travelling long-
haul, the best strategy is to buy a return ticket, say New York to
Bangkok and then take cheap flights or transport around Asia
and even to Australia and beyond.

Frequent Flyer Memberships

A frequent-flyer program (FFP) is a loyalty program offered by an airline. They are designed to encourage airline customers to fly more to accumulate points (also called miles, kilometres, or segments) which can be redeemed for air travel or other rewards.

You can sign up with any FFP program for free. There are three major airline alliances in the world: Oneworld, SkyTeam and Star Alliance. I am with One World https://www.oneworld.com/members because the points can be accrued and used for most flights.

The best return on your points is to use them for international business or first class flights with lie-flat seats. You would need 3 times more miles compared to an economy flight, but if you paid cash, you'd pay 5 - 10 times more than the cost of the economy flight, so it really pays to use your points only for upgrades. The worst value for your miles is to buy an economy seat or worse, a gift from the airlines gift-shop.

Sign up for a family/household account to pool miles together. If you share a common address you can claim the miles with most airlines. You can use AwardWallet to keep track of your miles. Remember that they only last for 2 years, so use them before they expire.

Pack like a Pro

"He who would travel happily must travel light." – Antoine de St. Exupery 59.

Travel as lightly as you can. We always need less than we think. You will be very grateful that you have a light pack when changing trains, travelling through the airport, catching a bus, walking to your accommodation, or climbing stairs.

Make a list of what you will wear for 7 days and take only those clothes. You can easily wash your things while you're travelling if you stay in an Airbnb with a washing machine or visit a local laundrette. Roll your clothes for maximum space usage and fewer wrinkles. If you feel really nervous about travelling with such few things make sure you have a dressier outfit, a little black dress for women is always valuable, a shirt for men. Then pack shorts, long pair of pants, loose tops and a hoodie to snuggle in. Remind yourself that a lack of clothing options is an opportunity to find bargain new outfits in thrift stores. You can either sell these on eBay after you've worn them or post them home to yourself. You'll feel less stressed, as you don't have to look after or feel weighed down by excess baggage. Here are three things to remember when packing:

- Co-ordinate colours - make sure everything you bring can be worn together.
- Be happy to do laundry - fresh clothes when you're travelling feels very luxurious.
- Take liquid minis no bigger than 60ml. Liquid is heavy and you simply don't need to carry so much at one time.

Checks to Avoid Fees

Always have 6 months validity on your passport

To enter most countries you need 6 months from the day you land. Factor in different time zones around the world if your passport is on the edge. Airport security will stop you from boarding your flight at the airport if your passport has 5 months and 29 days left.

Google Your Flight Number before you leave for the airport

Easily find out where your plane is from anywhere. Confirm the status of your flight before you leave for the airport with flightaware.com. This can save you long unnecessary wait times.

Check-in online

The founder, Ryan O'Leary of budget airline RyanAir famously said: "We think they should pay €60 for [failing to check-in on-line] being so stupid.". Always check-in online, even for international flights. Cheaper international carriers like Scoot will charge you at the airport to check-in.

Checking Bags

Never, ever check a bag if you possibly can avoid it. It is always cheaper to put heavier items on a ship, rather than take them on a flight with you. Find the best prices for shipping at https://www.parcelmonkey.com/delivery-services/shipping-heavy-items

Use a fragile sticker

Put a 'Fragile' sticker on anything you check to ensure that it's handled better as it goes through security. It'll also be one of the first bags released after the flight, getting you out of the airport quicker.

If you do check your bag, photograph it

Take a photo of your bag before you check it. This will speed up the paperwork if it is damaged or lost.

Relaxing at the airport

The best way to relax at the airport is in a lounge where they provide free food, drinks, comfortable chairs, luxurious amenities (many have showers) and if you're lucky a peaceful ambience. If you're there for a longer time look for Airport Cubicles, sleep pods which charge by the hour.

You can use your FFP Card (Frequent Flyer Memberships) to get into select lounges for free. Check your eligibility before you pay.

If you're travelling a lot I'd recommend to Invest in a Priority Pass for the airport.
It includes 850-plus airport lounges around the world. The cost is $99 for the year and $27 per lounge visit or you can pay $399 for the year all inclusive.

If you need a lounge pass for a one-off day, you can get a Day Pass. Buy it online for a discount, it always works out cheaper than buying at the airport. Use   .

Lounges are also great if you're travelling with kids, as they're normally free for kids and will definitely cost you less than snacks for your little ones. The rule is that kids should be seen and not heard, so consider this before taking an overly excited child who wants to run around, or you might be asked to leave even after you've paid.

Money: How to make it, spend it and save it while travelling

How to earn money WHILE travelling

"Twenty years from now you will be more disappointed by the things you didn't do than by the ones you did do. So throw off the bowlines. Sail away from the safe harbour." - H. Jackson Brown

Digital nomads receive a lot of hype. Put simply they are "professionals who work online and therefore don't need to tie themselves to one particular office, city, or even country."

The first step in becoming a digital nomad, earning money while travelling is knowing what you can offer. Your market is the whole world. So, what product or service would you like to offer that they would pay for? Take some time to think about this. In German, they say you should do whatever comes easily to your hand. For example, I've always loved finding bargains, it comes very easily for me. Yet I studied Law and Finance at University, which definitely did not come easy. It's no shock that it didn't transpire into a career. And served more as a lesson in not following my ego.

There are thousands of possibilities to generate income while travelling; offering services like tutorial, coaching, writing service pr blogging. Most travellers I meet try their hand at blogging and earning from the advertisements. This is great if you have some savings, but if you need to earn straight away to travel, this should be on the back burner, as it takes time to establish. Still if this comes easily to you, do it!

You want to make good money fast. Ask yourself, what is it that you are good at and how can you deliver maximum value to other people? Here are some ideas if you're totally dumfounded:

1. Teaching English online - you will need a private room for this. Be aware that if you're from the USA and the country you want to work in requires a federal-level background check, it

may take months, so apply early. Opportunities are on: t.vip-kid.com.cn, abc360.com, italki.com, verbalplanet.com and verbling.com. You can expect to earn $20 an hour.

2. Work in a hostel. Normally you'll get some cash and free accommodation.

3. Fruit picking. I picked Bananas in Tully Australia for $20 an hour. The jobs are menial but can be quite meditative. Look on WWOOF.org for organic farm work.

4. fiverr.com - offer a small service, like making a video template and changing the content for each buyer.

5. Do freelance work online: marketing, finance, writing, App creation, graphic designer, UX or UI designer, SEO optimizer / expert. Create a profile on upwork.com - you need to put in a lot of work to make this successful, but if you have a unique skill like coding, or marketing it can be very lucrative.

6. Make a udemy.com course. Can you offer a course in something people will pay for? e.g. stock trading, knitting or marketing.

7. Use skype to deliver all manner of services: language lessons, therapy, coaching etc. Google for what you could offer. Most specialisms have a platform you can use to find clients and they will take a cut of your earnings/ require a fee.

8. You could work on luxury yachts in the med. Its hard work, but you can save money - DesperateSailors.com

9. Become an Airbnb experience host - but this requires you to know one place and stay there for a time. And you will need a work visa for that country.

10. Work on a cruise ship. This isn't a digital nomad job but it will help you travel and save at the same time.

11. Rent your place out on airbnb while you travel and get a cleaner to manage it. The easiest solution if you own or have a long-term rent contract.

How to spend money

Budget travel hacking begins with a strategy to spend without fees. Your individual strategy depends greatly on the country you legally reside in as to what cards are available. Happily there are some fin-tech solutions which can save you thousands and are widely available globally. I will address those first:

N26

N26 is a 10-year old digital bank. I have been using them for over 6 years. The key advantage is fee-free card transactions abroad. They have a very elegant app, where you can check your timeline for all transactions listed in realtime or manage your in-app security anywhere. The card you receive is a Mastercard so you can use it everywhere. If you lose the card, you don't have to call anyone, just open the app and swipe 'lock card'. It puts your purchases into a graph automatically so you can see what you spend on. You can open an account from abroad entirely online, all you need is your passport and a camera

Revolut

Revolut is a multi-currency account that allows you to hold and exchange 29 currencies and spend fee-free abroad. It's a UK based neobank, but accepts customers from all over the world.

TransferWise debit card

If you're going to be in one place for a long time the The TransferWise debit card is like having your travel money on a card – it lets you spend money at the real exchange rate.

Monzo

Monzo is good if your UK based. They offer a fee-free UK account. Fee-free international money transfers and fee-free spending abroad.

The downside

The cards above are debit cards, meaning you need to have money in those accounts to spend it. This comes with one big downside: safety. Credit card issuers' have "zero liability" mean-

ing you're not liable for unauthorised charges. All of the cards listed above do provide cover for unauthorised charges but times vary greatly in how quickly you'd get your money back if it were stolen.

The best option is to check in your country to see which credit cards are the best for travelling and set up monthly payments to repay the whole amount so you don't pay unnecessary interest. In the USA, Schwab[1] regularly ranks at the top for travel credit cards. Credit cards are always the safer option when abroad simply because you get your money back faster if its stolen and if you're renting cars, most will give you free insurance when you book the car rental using the card, saving you money.

---

[1] Charles Schwab High Yield Checking accounts refund every single ATM fee worldwide, require no minimum balance and have no monthly fee.

Always withdraw money; never exchange.

Money exchanges whether they be on the streets or in the airports will NEVER give you a good exchange rate. Do not bring bundles of cash. Instead withdraw local currency from the ATM as needed and try to use only free ATM's. Many in airports charge you a fee to withdraw cash. Look for bigger ATM's attached to banks to avoid this.

Recap:

- Take cash from local, non-charging ATMs for the best rates.
- Never change at airport exchange desks unless you absolutely have to, then just change just enough to be able get to a bank ATM.
- Bring a spare credit card for emergencies.
- Split cash in various places on your person (pockets, shoes) and in your luggage. Its never sensible to keep your cash or cards all in one place.
- In higher risk areas, use a money belt under your clothes or put $50 in your shoe or bra.

How to save money while travelling

Saving money while travelling sounds like an oxymoron, but it can be done with little to no effort. Einstein is credited as saying, "Compound interest is the eighth wonder of the world." If you saved and invested $100 today, in 20 years it would be $2,000 thanks to the power of compound interest. It makes sense then to save your money, invest and make even more money.

The Acorns app is a simple system for this. It rounds up your credit card purchases and puts the rest into a savings account. So if you pay for a coffee and its $3.01, you'll save 0.99 cents. You won't even notice you're saving by using this app:

Here are some more generic ways you can always save money while travelling:

Device Safety
Having your phone, iPad or laptop stolen is one BIG and annoying way you can lose money traveling. The simple solution is to use apps to track your devices. Some OSes have this feature built-in. Prey will try your smartphones or laptops (preyproject.com).

Book New Airbnb's
When you take a risk on a new Airbnb listing, you save money. Just make sure the hosts profile is at least 3 years old and has reviews.

If you end up in an overcrowded city

The website   is like Airbnb for camping in people's garden and is a great way to save money if you end up in a city during a big event.

Look out for free classes
Lots of hostels offer free classes for guests. If you're planning to stay in a hostel, check out what classes your hostel offers. I have learnt languages, cooking techniques, dance styles, drawing and all manner of things for free by taking advantage of free classes at hostels.

Get a student discount card
If you're studying buy an ISIC card - International Student Identity Card. It is internationally recognised, valid in 133 countries and offers more than 150,000 discounts!

Instal
Maps me is extremely good for travelling without data. It's like offline google maps without the huge download size.

Always buy travel insurance
Don't travel without travel insurance. It is a small cost to pay compared with what could be a huge medical bill.

Travel Apps That'll Make Budget Travel Easier

Travel apps are useful for booking and managing travel logistics. They have one fatal downside, they can track you in the app and keep prices up. If you face this, access the site from an incognito browser tab.

Here are the best apps and what they can do for you:

- Best For flight Fare-Watching: Hopper.
- Best for booking flights: Skyscanner
- Best for timing airport arrivals: FlightAware - check on delays, cancellations and gate changes.
- Best for overcoming a fear of flying: SkyGuru - turbulence forecasts for the route you're flying.
- Best for sharing your location: TripWhistle - text or send your GPS coordinates or location easily.
- Best for splitting expenses among co-travellers: Splittr, Trip Splitter, Venmo or Splitwise.

We have covered the best apps and websites for Singapore in the section above called useful websites.

How NOT to be ripped off

"One of the great things about travel is that you find out how ma ny good, kind people there are."
— Edith Wharton

The quote above may seem ill placed in a chapter entitled how not to be ripped off, but I included it to remind you that the vast majority of people do not want to rip you off. In fact, scammers are normally limited to three situations:

1. Around heavily visited attractions - these places are targeted purposively due to sheer footfall. Many criminals believe ripping people off is simply a numbers game.
2. In cities or countries with low-salaries or communist ideologies. If they can't make money in the country, they seek to scam foreigners. If you have travelled to India, Morocco or Cuba you will have observed this phenomenon.
3. When you are stuck and the person helping you knows you have limited options.

Scammers know that most people will avoid confrontation. Don't feel bad about utterly ignoring someone and saying no. Here are six strategies to avoid being ripped off:

1. **Never ever agree to pay as much as you want. Always decide on a price before.**
Whoever you're dealing with is trained to tell you, they are uninterested in money. This is a trap. If you let people do this they will ask for MUCH MORE money at the end, and because you have used there service, you will feel obliged to pay. This is a con-man's trick and nothing more.

2. Pack light
You can move faster and easier. If you take heavy luggage you will end up taking taxi's which are comparatively very costly over time.

3. NEVER use the airport taxi service. Plan to use public transport before you reach the airport.

4. Don't buy a sim card from the airport. Buy from the local supermarkets it will cost 50% less.

5. Eat at local restaurants serving regional food
Food defines culture. Exploring all delights available to the palate doesn't need to cost huge sums.

6. Ask the locals what something should cost, and try not to pay over that.

7. If you find yourself with limited options. e.g. your taxi dumps you on the side of the road because you refuse to pay more (common in India and parts of South America) don't act desperate and negotiate as if you have other options or you will be extorted.

8. Don't blindly rely on social media

Let's say you post in a Facebook group that you want tips for travelling to The Maldives. A lot of the comments you will receive come from guides, hosts and restaurants doing their own promotion. It's estimated that 50% or more of Facebook's current monthly active users are fake[2]. And what's worse, a recent study found Social media platforms leave 95% of reported fake accounts up[3]. These accounts are the digital versions of the men who hang around the Grand Palace in Bangkok telling tourists its closed, to divert you to

---

[2]

[3]

shops where they will receive a commission for bringing you.

It can also be the case that genuine comments come from people who have totally different interests, beliefs and yes, budgets to yours. Make your experience your own and don't believe every comment you read.

Bottom line: use caution when accepting recommendations on social media and always fact-check with your own research.

Small tweaks on the road add up to big differences in your bank balance

Take advantage of other hotel's amenities

If you fancy a swim but you're nowhere near the ocean, try the nearest hotel with a pool. As long as you buy a drink, the hotel staff will likely grant you access.

Fill up your mini bar for free.

Fill up your mini bar for free by storing things from the breakfast bar or grocery shop in your mini bar to give you a greater selection of drinks and food without the hefty price tag.

Save yourself some ironing

Use the steam from the shower to get rid of wrinkles in clothing. If something is creased, leave it trapped with the steam in the bathroom overnight for even better results.

See somewhere else for free

Opt for long stopovers, allowing you to experience another city without spending much money.

Wear your heaviest clothes

on the plane to save weight in your pack, allowing you to bring more with you. Big coats can then be used as pillows to make your flight more comfortable.

Don't get lost while you're away.

Find where you want to go using Google Maps, then type 'OK Maps' into the search bar to store this information for offline viewing.

Use car renting services

Share Now or Car2Go allow you to hire a car for 2 hours for $25 in a lot of Europe.

Share Rides

Use sites like blablacar.com to find others who are driving in your direction. It can be 80% cheaper than normal transport. Just check the drivers reviews.

Use free gym passes

Get a free gym day pass by googling the name of a local gym and free day pass.

When asked by people providing you a service where you are from..

If there's no price list for the service you are asking for, when asked where you are from, Say you are from a lesser-known poorer country. I normally say Macedonia, and if they don't know where it is, add it's a poor country. If you say UK, USA, the majority of Europe bar the well-known poorer countries taxi drivers, tour operators etc will match the price to what they think you pay at home.

Set-up a New Uber/ other car hailing app account for discounts

By googling you can find offers with $50 free for new users in most cities for Uber/ Lyft/ Bolt and alike. Just set up a new gmail.com email account to take advantage.

Where and How to Make Friends

"People don't take trips, trips take people." – John Steinbeck

Become popular at the airport

Want to become popular at the airport? Pack a power bar with multiple outlets and just see how many friends you can make. It's amazing how many people forget their chargers, or who packed them in the luggage that they checked in.

Stay in Hostels

First of all, Hostels don't have to be shared dorms, and they cater to a much wider demographic than is assumed. Hostels are a better environment for meeting people than hotels, and more importantly they tended to open up excursion opportunities that further opened up that opportunity.

Or take up a hobby

If hostels are a definite no-no for you; find an interest. Take up a hobby where you will meet people. I've dived for years and the nature of diving is you're always paired up with a dive buddy. I met a lot of interesting people that way.

When unpleasantries come your way...

We all have our good and bad days travelling, and on a bad day you can feel like just taking a flight home. Here are some ways to overcome common travel problems:

Anxiety when flying

It has been over 40 years since a plane has been brought down by turbulence. Repeat that number to yourself: 40 years! Planes are built to withstand lighting strikes, extreme storms and ultimately can adjust course to get out of their way. Landing and take off are when the most accidents happen, but you have statistically three times the chance of winning a huge jackpot lottery, then you do of dying in a plane crash.

If you feel afraid on the flight focus on your breathing saying the word 'smooth' over and over until the flight is smooth. Always check the airline safety record on airlinerating.com I was surprised to learn Ryanair and Easyjet as much less safe than Wizz Air according to those ratings because they sell similarly priced flights. If there is extreme turbulence, I feel much better knowing I'm in a 7 star safety plane.

Wanting to sleep instead of seeing new places

This is a common problem. Just relax, there's little point do-ing fun things when you feel tired. Factor in jet-lag to your travel plans. When you're rested and alert you'll enjoy your new temporary home much more. Many people hate the first week of a long-trip because of jet-lag and often blame this on their first destination, but its rarely true. Ask travellers who 'hate' a particular place and you will see, that very often they either had jet-lag or an unpleasant journey there.

Going over budget

Come back from a trip to a monster credit card bill? Hopefully this guide has prevented you from returning to an unwanted bill. Of course, there are costs that can creep up and this is a reminder about how to prevent them making their way on to your credit card bill:

- To and from the airport. Solution: leave adequate time and take the cheapest method - book before.
- Baggage. Solution: take hand luggage and post things you might need to yourself.
- Eating out. Solution: go to cheap eats places and suggest those to friends.
- Parking. Solution: use apps to find free parking
- Tipping. Solution Leave a modest tip and tell the server you will write them a nice review.
- Souvenirs. Solution: fridge magnets only.
- Giving to the poor. (This one still gets me, but if you're giving away $10 a day - it adds up) Solution: volunteer your time instead and recognise that in tourist destinations many beggars are run by organised crime gangs.

Price v Comfort

I love traveling, I don't love struggling. I like decent accommodation, being able to eat properly and see places and enjoy. I am never in the mood for low cost airlines or crappy transfers so here's what I do to save money.

- Avoid organised tours unless you are going to a place where safety is a real issue. They are expensive and constrain your wanderlust to typical things. I only recommend them in Algeria, Iran and Papua New Guinea - where language and gender views pose serious problems all cured by a reputable tour organiser.
- Eat what the locals do.
- Cook in your airbnb/ hostel where restaurants are expensive.
- Shop at local markets.
- Spend time choosing your flight, and check the operator on arilineratings.com
- Mix up hostels and Airbnbs. Hostels for meeting people, Airbnb for relaxing and feeling 'at home'.

Not knowing where free toilets are

Use Toilet Finder - https://play.google.com/store/apps/details?id=com.bto.toilet&hl=en

Your airbnb is awful

Airbnb customer service is notoriously bad. Help yourself out. Try to sort things out with the host, but if you can't, take photos of everything e.g bed, bathroom, mess, doors, contact them within 24 hours. Tell them you had to leave and pay for new accommodation. Ask politely for a full refund including booking fees. With photographic evidence and your new accommodation receipt, they can't refuse.

The airline loses your bag

Go to the Luggage desk before leaving the airport and report the bag missing.
Most airlines will give you an overnight bag, ask where your staying and return the bag to you within three days. Its extremely rare for them to completely lose it due to technological innovation, but if that happens you should submit an insurance claim after the

three days is up, including receipts for everything your had to buy in the interim.

Your travel companion lets you down.

Whether it's a breakup or a friend cancelling, it sucks and can ramp up costs. The easiest solution to finding a new travel companion is to go to a well-reviewed hostel and find someone you want to travel with. You should spend at least three days getting to know this person before you suggest travelling together. Finding someone in person is always better than finding someone online, because you can get a better idea of whether you will have a smooth journey together. Travel can make or break friendships.

Culture shock

I had one of the strongest culture shocks while spending 6 months in Japan. It was overwhelming how much I had to prepare when I went outside of the door (googling words and sentences what to use, where to go, which station and train line to use, what is this food called in Japanese and how does its look etc.). I was so tired constantly but in the end I just let go and went with my extremely bad Japanese. If you feel culture shocked its because your brain is referencing your surroundings to what you know. Stop comparing, have Google translate downloaded and relax.

Your Car rental insurance is crazy expensive

I always use carrentals.com and book with a credit card. Most credit cards will give you free insurance for the car, so you don't need to pay the extra.

You're sick

First off ALWAYS, purchase travel insurance. Including emergency transport up to $500k even to back home, which is usually less than $10 additional. I use https://www.comparethemarket.com/travel-insurance/ to find the best days. If I am sick I normally check into a hotel with room service and ride it out.

Make a Medication Travel Kit

Take travel sized medications with you:

- Antidiarrheal medication (for example, bismuth subsalicylate, loperamide)
- Medicine for pain or fever (such as acetaminophen, aspirin, or ibuprofen)
- Throat Lozenges

Save yourself from most travel related hassles

- Do not make jokes with immigration and customs staff. A misunderstanding can lead to HUGE fines.

- Book the most direct flight you can find, nonstop if possible.

- Carry a US$50 bill for emergency cash. I have entered a country and all ATM and credit card systems were down. US$ can be exchanged nearly anywhere in the world and is useful in extreme situations, but where possible don't exchange, as you will lose money.

- Check, and recheck, required visas and such BEFORE the day of your trip. Some countries, for instance, require a ticket out of the country in order to enter. Others, like the

US and Australia, require electronic authorisation in advance.

- Airport security is asinine and inconsistent around the world. Keep this in mind when connecting flights. Always leave at least 2 hours for international connections or international to domestic. In London Stansted for example, they force you to buy one of their plastic bags, and remove your liquids from your own plastic bag.... just to make money from you. And this adds to the time it will take to get through security so lines are long.

- Wiki travel is perfect to use for a lay of the land.

- Expensive luggage rarely lasts longer than cheap luggage, in my experience. Fancy leather bags are toast with air travel.
-

Food

- When it comes to food, eat in local restaurants, not tourist-geared joints. Any place with the menu in three or more languages is going to be overpriced.
- Take a spork - a knife, spoon and fork all in one.

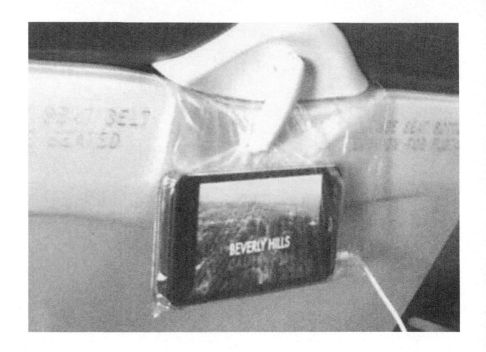

Water Bottle

Take a water bottle with a filter. We love these ones from Water to Go.
Empty it before airport security and separate the bottle and filter as some airport people will try and claim it has liquids…

Bug Sprays

If you're heading somewhere tropical spray your clothes with Permethrin before you travel. It lasts 40 washes and saves space in your bag. A 'Bite Away' zapper can be used after the bite to totally erase it. It cuts down on the itching and erases the bite from your skin.

Order free mini's

Don't buy those expensive travel sized toiletries, order travel sized freebies online. This gives you the opportunity to try brands you've never used before, and who knows, you might even find your new favourite soap.

Take a waterproof bag

If you're travelling alone you can swim without worrying about your phone, wallet and passport laying on the beach. You can also use it as a source of entertainment on those ultra budget flights.

Make a private entertainment centre anywhere

Always take an eye-mask, earplugs, a scarf and a kindle reader - so you can sleep and entertain yourself anywhere!

The best Travel Gadgets

The door alarm

If you're nervous and staying in private rooms or airbnbs take a door alarm. For those times when you just don't feel safe, it can help you fall asleep. You can get tiny ones for less than $10 from Amazon:

Smart Blanket

Amazon sells a 6 in 1 heating blanket that is very useful for cold plane or bus trips. Its great if you have poor circulation as it becomes a detachable Foot Warmer: Amazon http:// amzn.to/2hTYlOP I paid $49.00.

The coat that becomes a tent

https://www.adiff.com/products/tent-jacket. This is great if you're going to be doing a lot of camping.

Clever Tank Top with Secret Pockets

Keep your valuables safe in this top. Perfect for all climates.

on Amazon for $39.90

Optical Camera Lens for Smartphones and Tablets
Leave your bulky camera at home. Turn your device into a high-performance camera. Buy on Amazon for $9.95

Travel-sized Wireless Router with USB Media Storage

Convert any wired network to a wireless network. Buy on Amazon for $17.99

Buy a Scrubba Bag to wash your clothes on the go
Or a cheaper imitable. You can wash your clothes on the go.

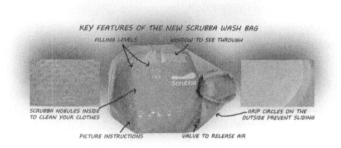

Hacks for Families

Rent an Airbnb apartment so you can cook

Apartments are much better for families, as you have all the amenities you'd have at home. They are normally cheaper per person too. We are the first travel guide publisher to include Airbnb's in our recommendations if you think any of these need updating you can email me at philgtang@gmail.com

Shop at local markets

Eat seasonal products and local products. Get closer to the local market and observe the prices and the offer. What you can find more easily, will be the cheapest

Take Free Tours

Download free podcast tours of the destination you are visiting. The podcast will tell you where to start, where to go, and what to look for. Often you can find multiple podcast tours of the same place. Listen to all of them if you like, each one will tell you a little something new.

Pack Extra Ear Phones

If you go on a museum tour, they often have audio guides. Instead of having to rent one for each person, take some extra earphones. Most audio tour devices have a place to plug in a second set.

Buy Souvenirs Ahead of Time

If you are buying souvenirs, something touristy, you are paying a premium price. By ordering the exact same product online from sites like Aliexpress.com, you save a lot of money and hassle. You can have them shipped to your home address so you don't have to carry them around, but still have something to give friends and family when you return.

Use Cheap Transportation

Do as the locals do, including checking out weekly passes.

Carry Reusable Water Bottles

Spending money on water and other beverages can quickly add up. Instead of paying for drinks, take some refillable water bottles.

Combine Attractions

Many major cities offer ticket bundles where one price gets you into 5 or 6 popular attractions. You will need to plan ahead of time to decide what things you plan to do on vacation and see if they are selling these activities together.

Pack Snacks

Granola bars, apples, baby carrots, bananas, cheese crackers, juice boxes, pretzels, fruit snacks, apple sauce, grapes, and veggie chips.

Stick to Carry-On Bags

Do not pay to check a large bag. Even a small child can pull a carry-on.

Visit free art galleries and museums

Just google the name + free days.

Eat Street Food

There's a lot of unnecessary fear around this. You can watch the food prepared. Go for the stands that have a steady queue.

Travel Gadgets for Families

Dropcam

Are what-if scenarios playing out in your head? Then you need Dropcam.

'Dropcam HD Internet Wi-Fi Video Monitoring Cameras help you watch what you love from anywhere. In less than a minute, you'll have it setup and securely streaming video to you over your home Wi-Fi. Watch what you love while away with Dropcam HD.'

Approximate Price: $139

Kelty-Child-Carrier

Voted as one of the best hiking essentials if you're traveling with kids and can carry a child up to 18kg.

Jetkids Bedbox

No more giving up your own personal space on the plane with this suitcase that becomes a bed.

Safety

"If you think adventure is dangerous, try routine. It's lethal." – Paulo Coelho

Backpacker murdered is a media headline that leads people to think traveling is more dangerous than it is. The media sensationalise the rare murders and deaths of backpackers and travellers. The actual chances of you dying abroad are extremely extremely low.

Let's take the USA as an example. In 2018, 724 Americans **died** from unnatural causes, 167 died from car accidents, while the majority of the other deaths resulted from drownings, suicides, and non-vehicular accidents. Contrast this with the 15,000 murders in the US in 2018, and travelling abroad looks much safer than staying at home.

There are many thing you can to keep yourself save. Here are out tips.

1. Always check fco.co.uk before travelling. NEVER RELY on websites or books. Things are changing constantly and the FCO's (UK's foreign office) advice is always UP TO DATE (hourly) and extremely conservative.
2. Check your mindset. I've travelled alone to over 180 countries and the main thing I learnt is if you walk around scared, or anticipating you're going to be pickpocketed, your constant fear will attract bad energy. Murders or attacks on travellers are the mainstay of media, not reality, especially in countries familiar with travellers. The only place I had cause to genuinely fear for my life was Papa New Guinea - where nothing actually happened to me only my own panic over culture shock.

There are many things you can do to stop yourself being victim to the two main problems when travelling: theft or being scammed.

I will address theft first. Here are my top tips:

- Stay alert while you're out and always have an exit strategy.
- Keep your money in a few different places on your person and your passport somewhere it can't be grabbed.
- Take a photo of your passport on your phone incase. If you do lose it, google for your embassy, you can usually get a temporary pretty fast.
- Google safety tips for traveling in your country to help yourself out and memorise the emergency number.
- At hostels keep your large bag in the room far under the bed/ out of the way with a lock on the zipper.
- On buses/trains I would even lock my bag to the luggage rack.
- Get a personal keychain alarm. The sound will scare anyone away.
- Don't wear any jewellery. A man attempted to rob a friend of her engagement ring in Bogota, Colombia, and in hindsight I wished I'd told her to leave it at home/wear it on a hidden necklace, as the chaos it created was avoidable.
- Don't turn your back to traffic while you use your phone.
- When traveling in the tuktuk sit in the middle and keep your bag secure. Wear sunglasses as dust can easily get in your eyes.
- Don't let anyone give you flowers, bracelets, or any type of trinket, even if they insist it's for free and compliment you like crazy.
- Don't let strangers know that you are alone - unless they are travel friends ;-)
- Lastly, and most importantly -Trust your gut! If it doesn't feel right, it isn't.

Hilarious Travel Stories

I have compiled these short stories from fellow travellers to pick you up when you're feeling down. Life on the road isn't always easy and we've all had those days when we want to stay in bed and forget the world exists. Laughter is the best way I know to shake those feelings. All people who have shared these stories wanted to remain anonymous. After reading them I think you'll understand why…

I mentioned my wife earlier, so its only fair she be the first story. Don't worry she has given me permission to share.

A marriage up the wall

'Delhi belly got me on the third day into the trip to India. I was vomiting so much that I couldn't keep even water down so I went to a health clinic for tourists. Whilst I was there I was asked to poop into a jar and happily put on a drip.

The doctor attending me was mid to late 40's and very creepy. I decided I'd leave the clinic after my 4th bag of fluids because I felt better and was weirded out by the intense stares of my doctor. As I was paying the bill, the doctor came over, dropped to one knee and asked me to marry him at the desk. I stuttered in shock that I was already was married. He was holding a jar of my poo in his hand, stood and then chucked it at the wall. The jar broke open and my watery specimen was literally smeared across the wall as he trudged off. The woman serving me bobbed her head from side to side as if we were discussing the weather and said 'its not personal madam, you look like his last wife.'

Glass shame

'I was in Nashville airport in the smoking room. I heard my name being called for my flight so I rushed out but instead of rushing through the door, I walked smack into the glass. When I opened the door the entire departure lounge was roaring with laughter.'

The Dashing Date

'I had a date with a fellow Brit in Medellin. I went to the bathroom and when I came back, I asked him if he had paid the bill and he replied 'yes'. We were going down some stairs when he suddenly shouted at me to run. Yes, the restaurant staff were running after us because he hadn't paid.'

A fear of farting in hostels

'When I arrived to stay in my first ever hostel in London, I realised I had an intense fear
farting in my sleep. I literally gave myself such bad constipation I had to go to hospital. It turns out an enema is worse than hostel farting.'

What a boob

I fell on the Tube in London getting into a carriage. Unfortunately I managed to grab a woman's boob on the way to the floor. I was so mortified I walked everywhere else during the trip.'

Cementing a few laughs

'I was walking on the streets in Singapore when they were fixing the roads. I somehow stepped in fresh cement. I only noticed when my feet became so heavy I thought I had twisted my ankle. The cement got so hard, I had to take my shoes off as I couldn't pick up my feet. Locals were very clearly entertained as I walked back to my accommodation in my sponge bob squarepants socks.

If you've got a hilarious travel story you'd love to share, email me at   **. All identifying details will be removed.**

How I got hooked on budget travelling

'We're on holiday' is what my dad used to say to justify getting us in so much debt we lost our home and all our things when I was 11. We moved from the suburban bliss of Hemel Hempstead to a run down council estate in inner-city London, near my dad's new job as a refuge collector, a fancy word for dustbin man. I lost all my school friends while watching my dad go through a nervous breakdown.

My dad loved walking up a hotel lobby desk without a care in the world. So much so, that he booked overpriced holidays on credit cards. A lot of holidays. As it turned out we couldn't afford any of them. In the end, my dad had no choice but to declare bankruptcy. When my mum realised he'd racked up so much debt our family unit dissolved. A neat and perhaps as painless a summary of events that lead me to my life's passion: budget travel that doesn't compromise on fun, safety or comfort.

I started travelling full-time at the age of 18. I wrote the first Super Cheap Insider guide for friends visiting Norway - which I did for a month on less than $250. When sales reached 10,000 I decided to form the Super Cheap Insider Guides company. As I know from first-hand experience debt can be a noose around our necks, and saying 'oh come on, we're on vacation' isn't a get out of jail free card.

Before I embarked upon writing Super Cheap Insider guides many, many people told me that my dream was impossible, travelling on a budget could never be comfortable. I hope this guide has proved to you what I have known for a long-time: budget travel can feel luxurious when you know and use the insider hacks.

And apologies, if I depressed you with my tale of woe. My dad is now happily remarried and works as a chef in London at a fancy hotel - the kind he used to take us to!

A final word...

There's a simple system you can use to think about budget travel. In life we can choose two of the following: cheap, fast or quality. So if you want it Cheap and fast you will get a lower quality service. Fast-food is the perfect example. The system holds true for purchasing anything while travelling. I always choose cheap and quality, except in times where I am really limited on time. Normally you can make small tweaks to make this work for you. Ultimately you must make choices about what's most important to you.

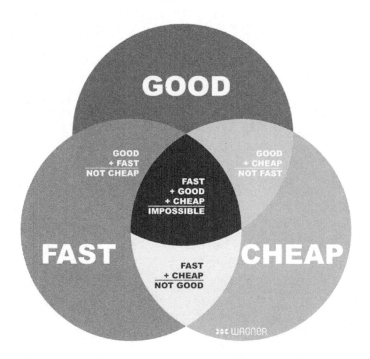

Our Writers

Phil Tang was born in London to immigrants, Phil graduated from The London School of Economics with a degree in Law. Now he travels full-time in search of travel bargains with his wife, dog and 1 year old daughter.

Ali Blythe has been writing about amazing places for 17 years. He loves travel and especially tiny budgets equalling big adventures nearly as much as his family. He recently trekked the Satopanth Glacier trekking through those ways from where no one else would trek. Ali is an adventurer by nature and bargainist by religion.

Michele Whitter writes about languages and travel. What separates her from other travel writers is her will to explain complex topics in a no-nonsense, straightforward way. She doesn't promise the world. But always delivers step-by-step methods you can immediately implement to travel on a budget.

Kim Mortimer, Kim's input on Super Cheap Insider Guides show you how to stretch your money further so you can travel cheaper, smarter, and with more wanderlust. She loves going over land on horses and helps us refine each guide to keep them effective.

Congratulations, you've saved money and done Good!

We donate 10% of all book profits to charity.

This year we are donating to Animal Shelters including one in Singapore. I'm sure you've seen your fair share of abandoned dogs during your travels: its heart wrenching to see man's best friend starving and alone.

'My dog Gracie was abandoned on the highway in Slovakia. At just ten months old, they tied her to the railings and left her there. Animal Hope picked her up and took care of her and found her a home with us. She is now a healthy, happy girl and loves travelling with us, getting her nose into new smells and soliciting belly rubs from fellow travellers. What breaks my heart is her 'I haven't been abandoned dance'. She is always so happy that we haven't abandoned her when we collect her from outside a supermarket that she dances on her leash for several minutes. Watch her 'I haven't been abandoned dance' dance ⸱ Money could never buy the happiness she has brought my family and me, but donations can help other abandoned animals like her to find loving homes.'

Katherine Huber, a contributor to Super Cheap Vienna.

Donations are made on the 4th January of each year on profits from the previous year. To nominate a charity to receive 10% of the proceeds of sales from our 2021 editions complete the form here: supercheapinsiderguides.com

Gracie

Copyright

Published in Great Britain in 2019 by Super Cheap Insider Guides LTD.